OUTDOOR EDUCATION IN GIRL SCOUTING

Girl Scouts of the U.S.A./830 Third Avenue/New York, N.Y. 10022

 GIRL SCOUTS OF THE U.S.A.

Mrs. Orville L. Freeman, *President*
Frances Hesselbein, *National Executive Director*

Inquiries related to *Outdoor Education in Girl Scouting* should be directed to Program, Girl Scouts of the U.S.A., 830 Third Avenue, New York, N.Y. 10022.

Authors

Candace White Ciraco	Corinne M. Murphy
Gayle E. Davis	Donna L. Nye
Joan W. Fincutter	Verna L. Simpkins
Sharon Woods Hussey	Karen M. White
Carolyn L. Kennedy	

. . . and a special acknowledgment to Mabel A. Hammersmith and Edith Loe

Girl Scout Catalog No. 26-217
ISBN 0-88441-454-X

10   9   8   7

Contents

Introduction

Do you remember a time when you stepped outdoors and truly discovered the joy and beauty of the world around you? A time when you paused to watch a beautiful sunset? Watched a young child touch and smell a flower for the first time? Smiled as a sandpiper's legs became a blur as the bird raced away from an oncoming wave? The thrill and excitement you experienced can be relived each time you share outdoor experiences with a child. Although primarily designed for the Girl Scout leader who wishes to explore the out-of-doors with a group of Junior Girl Scouts, *Outdoor Education in Girl Scouting* can be used by Cadette and Senior Girl Scouts. In fact, Girl Scout leaders of Brownie and Daisy Girl Scouts will find that many activities in this book can be enjoyed by younger Girl Scouts.

Outdoor Education in Girl Scouting is divided into three sections: Camping and Campcraft Skills; Girl Scout Ceremonies; and Outdoor Education Activities in the Five Worlds of Interest.

Camping and Campcraft Skills describes basic camping skills and provides such information as how to determine a girl's readiness for camping, how to remain safe and healthy in the out-of-doors, and how to select and care for camping equipment. The Girl Scout Ceremonies section describes a range of ceremonies from simple troop ceremonies that can be performed in a local park to a Girl Scouts' Own inspired by an outdoor theme. The Outdoor Education Activities in the Five Worlds of Interest section is divided into the five worlds and includes activities for indoors and out—all designed to enhance an appreciation and understanding of the out-of-doors.

A Quality Outdoor Experience

Space-age fabrics, foods, and lightweight metals, all produced at relatively low cost, have revolutionized the types of clothing and equipment available for outdoor recreation activities. Thus, a wide range of activities can be done in the out-of-doors. At the same time, open space near population centers is being consumed by development. We must, therefore, look at our outdoor pursuits with new insight—our activities must touch the Earth lightly, leaving as few traces of our presence as possible. A quality outdoor experience can be provided for the girls of today and tomorrow if each activity impacts the land minimally.

Outdoor activities have always been an integral part of Girl Scouting. Juliette Low knew that girls would be attracted to the out-of-doors for sports, camping, and nature study. That vision dispelled the notion of her day that ladies do nothing more strenuous than "sit on a cushion and sew a fine seam."

Definition of Outdoor Education

Today, outdoor education is defined as the effective utilization of Girl Scout program in the outdoor setting to enable girls to grow with regard to each of the four Girl Scout program goals. The primary approach should be experiential learning. Through the five Girl Scout worlds of interest, outdoor education enhances understanding and skill development of girls as well as aiding development of outdoor recreation interests. Outdoor education also creates an appreciation of the human relationship with the environment and, while developing skills for creative use of leisure time, teaches the importance of minimal impact to the environment.

Outdoor activities should help each girl:

- develop herself to achieve her full individual potential.
- relate to others with increasing understanding, skill, and respect.
- develop values to guide her actions and to provide the foundation for sound decision-making.
- contribute to the improvement of society through the use of her abilities and leadership skills, working in cooperation with others.

Girls today are involved in many different outdoor activities. Girl Scout councils across the country make available a wide variety of resources to enhance outdoor education. These resources include leader training; equipment; outdoor sites and facilities that meet Girl Scout, state, and local standards; and planned outdoor activities for girls. These activities may include wider opportunities of all kinds as well as day camping, resident camping, troop camping, day activities, and festivals.

Camping experiences and facilities are an important part of outdoor education because they provide a 24-hour-a-day atmosphere where each individual is challenged to grow physically, mentally, socially, and spiritually. Girl Scout camping is different from other outdoor experiences because it is a group effort—the girls involved have planned their own activities, meals, and schedules to meet their own needs.

What are the needs of girls today?

1. Each girl needs to feel accepted by the group and regarded with affection by others.

2. She needs to feel a sense of achievement and control over her activities.

3. She needs to feel secure, free from physical as well as social harm.

4. She needs opportunities for new adventures—exciting and varied activities to test the limits of her skills and to enable her to feel a sense of accomplishment.

5. She needs recognition and approval—to stand out as an individual for the things she does well.

6. She needs to share and enjoy leisure-time activities with a positive adult role model.

Girl Scout camping is the creative, educational experience in group living in the out-of-doors that makes all this happen.

Progression in Outdoor Activities

As you, the leader, discuss with girls the activities they wish to plan for the future, you may find girls with no interest in outdoor pursuits and girls who just can't wait for the next outdoor activity! For girls with little outdoor experience, start with activities in the most familiar outdoor environment before venturing far from home. Girl Scout program is built on the concept of progression, that is, acquiring the skills needed to progress to more difficult or highly skilled activities. Progressive outdoor experiences can be planned farther and farther away from home as girls build their confidence and skills. For instance, if part of an upcoming troop meeting will be spent outdoors, girls should prepare by discussing which clothing is comfortable to wear for outdoor activities and the behavior expected of each girl and the group in the out-of-doors. The World of the Out-of-Doors Dabbler badge described in

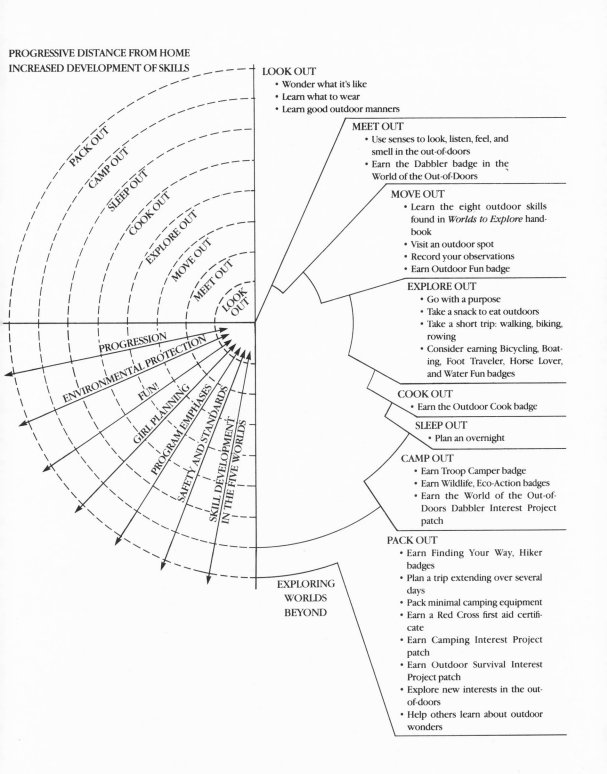

PROGRESSIVE DISTANCE FROM HOME
INCREASED DEVELOPMENT OF SKILLS

PACK OUT
CAMP OUT
SLEEP OUT
COOK OUT
EXPLORE OUT
MOVE OUT
MEET OUT
LOOK OUT

PROGRESSION
ENVIRONMENTAL PROTECTION
FUN!
GIRL PLANNING
PROGRAM EMPHASES
SAFETY AND STANDARDS
SKILL DEVELOPMENT IN THE FIVE WORLDS

LOOK OUT
- Wonder what it's like
- Learn what to wear
- Learn good outdoor manners

MEET OUT
- Use senses to look, listen, feel, and smell in the out-of-doors
- Earn the Dabbler badge in the World of the Out-of-Doors

MOVE OUT
- Learn the eight outdoor skills found in *Worlds to Explore* handbook
- Visit an outdoor spot
- Record your observations
- Earn Outdoor Fun badge

EXPLORE OUT
- Go with a purpose
- Take a snack to eat outdoors
- Take a short trip: walking, biking, rowing
- Consider earning Bicycling, Boating, Foot Traveler, Horse Lover, and Water Fun badges

COOK OUT
- Earn the Outdoor Cook badge

SLEEP OUT
- Plan an overnight

CAMP OUT
- Earn Troop Camper badge
- Earn Wildlife, Eco-Action badges
- Earn the World of the Out-of-Doors Dabbler Interest Project patch

PACK OUT
- Earn Finding Your Way, Hiker badges
- Plan a trip extending over several days
- Pack minimal camping equipment
- Earn a Red Cross first aid certificate
- Earn Camping Interest Project patch
- Earn Outdoor Survival Interest Project patch
- Explore new interests in the out-of-doors
- Help others learn about outdoor wonders

EXPLORING WORLDS BEYOND

Girl Scout Badges and Signs can serve as a springboard to a variety of outdoor activities.

The skills described under Camping and Campcraft Skills will help you and the girls take the next steps to exciting outdoor adventures. When girls have learned the skills to live comfortably in the out-of-doors, other aspects of outdoor living can be enjoyed. Backpacking, hiking, and boating, for example, can be sampled in different seasons and in diverse regions of the country (state and national parks). New methods of travel (horseback, bicycle, canoe, backpacking) can be experienced. And, the fascinating interrelationship of water, soil, air, plants, and animals can be discovered.

To provide the most effective outdoor experiences for girls, the following points should be considered.

- In order to have maximum impact on the lives of girls, activities should take place in the out-of-doors.

- Skills are best learned when practiced directly by each girl, not by watching others or reading about them.

- Use authentic objects. Touch and smell a leaf; learn more about its shape from a book.

- Teach the interrelationship of elements in the out-of-doors; for example, discuss how outdoor activities impact the land, or how birds depend on trees for food and shelter.

- Use a multisensory approach. Encourage girls to use as many senses as possible in each activity. The smell of food cooking outdoors is a familiar scent, but have you stopped to smell fresh earth, a wildflower, or the air after a rainstorm?

- Activities should provide built-in motivation. They should be fun, challenging, and different from activities done elsewhere and should focus on individual interests and first-hand experiences.

- Activities should have minimal impact on the natural environment. If you backpack into a campsite, pack out all your leftover food and trash. Remove all evidence of your presence.

- In terms of promoting a positive attitude in girls and a strengthened girl/adult partnership, planning an activity is as important as doing the activity itself.

- There should be opportunities for each girl to challenge herself. The out-of-doors provides a wide variety of opportunities for challenge within the health and safety standards of Girl Scout program.

- Just because a group of people are camping together does not mean that positive relationships will necessarily result. The adult role model is very important in setting a positive tone for the group.

- The outdoor setting has tremendous potential for developing and enhancing positive relationships, but it must be recognized that certain experiences and settings do not "speak to" the needs of certain individuals. Therefore, a variety of choices, which appeals to all girls, must be supplied.

- Outdoor activities will have the greatest impact on the behavior and values of those girls who are afforded the greatest number of opportunities to participate. Significant attitude changes occur in girls who have had at least three to five outdoor experiences (depending on the age of the girl). Both quality and quantity of outdoor experiences count!

- Those who develop the deepest appreciation of interrelationships in the environment are usually those who have had many opportunities to experience the natural world.

The Metric System

The measurements in this book are metric, with the U.S. system of measurement indicated in parentheses. The metric system is used by scientists and in most other countries. For those who need a refresher, here are some helpful comparisons:

A meter (m) is the distance from the fingertips of an adult's outstretched arm to the opposite shoulder. In the metric system, based on tens, a meter is divided into 100 centimeters.

A centimeter (cm) is the width of a large paper clip.

On the Celsius (C) temperature scale, water freezes at 0° C and boils at 100° C. In winter, rooms are heated to about 20° C; on a hot summer day, the thermometer might read 30° C. Normal human body temperature is 37° C.

Liquids are measured in milliliters (ml). One milliliter is equivalent to five drops of water squeezed from an eye-dropper. A liter (l) contains 1,000 milliliters and is slightly more than a quart.

Mass is measured in grams (g). One gram is about equal to the weight of a paper clip. A U.S. dime weighs two grams. A kilogram (kg) equals 1,000 grams. A one-liter volume of water weighs a kilogram.

Camping and Campcraft Skills

Girl Scout Camping Defined

Girl Scout camping is an experience that provides a creative, educational opportunity in group living in the out-of-doors. Its purpose is to utilize Girl Scout program, trained leadership, and the resources of natural surroundings to contribute to each camper's mental, physical, social, and spiritual growth.

This group living experience could include troop/group camping, core staff camping, day and resident camping, family camping, travel and trip camping. Definitions of these terms are found in the glossary. Check with the local Girl Scout council for guidelines on these types of camping.

Readiness

The first night away from home on a Girl Scout camping trip is a big step for most girls. A girl needs to be emotionally ready for this experience and should have a genuine desire to go camping. Certain skills are necessary for a camping trip that would make the girl's experience more enjoyable. These skills can be developed through activities at the troop meeting place or at home.

Girls with disabilities may not meet many of the readiness criteria indicated below. However, modifications in the camping experience can enable girls with disabilities to enjoy camping. Modifications may include camping at a facility accessible to girls with physical limitations, inviting additional adults such as parents or teachers to help supervise, bringing girls with more camping experience to help work with these campers, or shortening the length of the trip for girls who may not be emotionally ready for several days away from home.

The readiness indicators that follow are not meant to be a set of requirements that need to be fulfilled before a girl can go camping. Instead, they are included as a guide of points to consider when making the initial decision to go camping.

1. She wants to go.

2. She is not afraid to be away from home or parents overnight (and parents are prepared to let their daughter go).

3. She is willing to sleep, eat, and play with all girls, not just with best friends.

4. She can cope with unknowns:
   a. strange places (including latrines)
   b. darkness (no electricity)
   c. woods; night noises
   d. insects and other small creatures

5. She can manage with little or no privacy.

6. She doesn't always have to have her own way; she can give in graciously.

7. She can function as a member of a group.

The following indicators can be used as a guide in determining whether or not a girl possesses the necessary skills and knowledge to enjoy camping. Many of these skills can be learned before the trip or at the campsite.

1. She has satisfactorily followed instructions previously and can cooperate in planning a simple trip.

2. She can follow a kaper chart or similar assignment sheet.

3. She can follow written or verbal instructions for food preparation.

4. She can wash dishes, clean up kitchen/cooking area, and store food properly.

5. She can make a bed.

6. She has been on a series of day trips, cookouts, or has gone family camping overnight.

7. She has demonstrated (practiced) necessary skills in troop meetings: packing and repacking her luggage, rolling and tying a bedroll, operating a flashlight, lantern, etc.

Preparation

Before girls and adults ever reach the campsite, decisions must be made and preparations completed. Careful planning will result in a successful, coordinated camping experience and offers the perfect forum for encouraging and developing strong girl/adult partnerships.

First, decide which type of camping the girls would like to do. Refer to the different types of camping mentioned on page 10 and in the glossary. Remember, the type of camping chosen and the length of stay decided upon will depend greatly upon the troop's readiness.

Consider the following questions to determine the type of camping to choose:

- Are the girls ready for camping in a tent or would a cabin be better?
- Are the girls physically strong enough and are they coordinated enough to set up a tent?
- Are the girls ready to cook over an open fire or portable stove, or would a gas or electric range be better for them?
- Do the girls have prior camping experience?

Where to Camp

Once the type of camping has been chosen, decide where to camp by checking with the local Girl Scout council and local parks department. Suggestions also may be available through other youth-serving agencies in your area.

Some of the other considerations that must be addressed before the trip are:

- How will you get there?
- What kind of food will you bring and how much?
- How will you store the food once you arrive on the site?
- How will you finance the trip?
- How many adults will be needed and who will they be? Have these adults completed the required training given by the local Girl Scout council?
- Which supplies will be needed? (See the camping equipment checklist.)
- Which Girl Scout program activities will be done while camping?

Kaper Charts

The jobs that need to be done while camping, such as cooking, setting the table, and cleaning up, are called kapers and are listed on a kaper chart.

The kaper chart is usually drawn up before the camping trip so that everyone knows which jobs need to be done and who will do them.

The easiest way to divide up the camp jobs is for the troop/group to work together as patrols, in pairs, or in committees. Jobs can be rotated among the patrols so that everyone has a chance to do each of the different jobs.

Your group's kaper chart could look like this:

	MON	TUE	WED	THUR	FRI	SAT
COOK	flower	duck	owl	star	star	flower
FIRE	star	flower	duck	owl	star	star
WATER	star	star	flower	duck	owl	star
SETTING TABLE	owl	star	star	flower	duck	owl
CLEAN UP	duck	owl	star	star	flower	duck

Or like this:

Bring along only those items necessary for the type of camping you will be doing. Determine what equipment is available at the campsite that can be used by your group. Acquaint every girl and adult attending the trip with all the equipment they may be using.

Consider the following equipment checklist to determine which items to bring.

Shelter
* tents
* tent repair kit—including needle and nylon thread and tape or adhesive fabric
* kitchen or dining fly (canvas canopy)
* tarpaulins or plastic sheeting—to cover a woodpile, make a shelter, or enclose a latrine or shower.

Tools/Supplies
* hammer or mallet
* shovel
* can opener
* flashlight or lantern
* knife
* compass
* wire
* rope
* sharpening stone
* first aid kit—see Security, Safety, and Health in the Out-of-Doors, in this section, for specific items to include.

Cooking Equipment
* pots and pans with lids—when selecting utensils, consider the type of heat source to be used and the food that will be prepared.
* matches in a waterproof container
* potholders
* portable stove
* containers for leftover food
* grate—when cooking over a fire, it provides stable support for pots.
* a large knife, a spatula, measuring cups, forks, knives, and spoons (include some utensils with long handles)
* plastic garbage bags

Safety Tip—Bring a large pot or pail that can be filled with water and used as a fire bucket near the fire.

Washing Supplies

- dishpan or pail
- sponge or cloth
- towel for drying pots
- dishwashing soap
- net bags for air drying dishes
- scouring powder
- plastic or rubber gloves
- washbasins, if necessary
- tub or pail to heat water for washing

Personal Equipment Checklist

Select clothing based on the weather and location of your camping trip. Review the following checklist before packing.

- pants and shorts
- shirts
- sweaters and sweatshirts—several lightweight sweaters are warmer than one heavy sweater.
- sleepwear
- underwear
- socks
- sneakers, hiking shoes, or boots
- jacket—weight depends on season and weather.
- gloves
- hat—for sun and/or warmth depending on conditions.
- rain gear—waterproof raincoat or poncho, boots, and hat
- personal hygiene items—soap, shampoo, towel, wash-cloth, toothbrush, toothpaste, comb, brush, deodorant, sanitary napkins
- bedroll or sleeping bag and plastic ground cover for bedding.
- duffel bag for carrying personal equipment
- mess kit that includes silverware, plate, bowl, and cup
- canteen or water bottle
- flashlight
- dunk bag (nylon mesh for dishes)
- prescribed medication—should be placed in the first aid kit and administered by an adult.

Emergency Preparedness

Being prepared is the safest and smartest way to prevent accidents and handle emergencies. Key points to remember and prepare for before the camping trip can help ensure a good experience.

Before leaving on the camping trip, a list of girls and adults going on the trip should be left with at least two emergency contact persons at home or at the local Girl Scout council, if required. This list should include a complete address, telephone number, and two emergency contacts for each person. Names of parents/guardians should be listed for each girl. The emergency contact persons also should have a complete itinerary of the trip, including: a telephone number for the site, Girl Scout council emergency information, a map of the site with any proposed side trips, the route taken (the return trip, if different), and an approximate timetable for departures and arrivals. Parents/guardians should be instructed to contact one of the emergency contact persons for any information during the time of the trip. The contact person will notify the parents/guardians in the event of delays or changes in the original itinerary.

The site should be checked ahead of time to learn the location and telephone number of the police station, fire department, rescue squad or ambulance service, and civil defense center; the route to the nearest hospital; and any other emergency information. Make sure you have the name and telephone number of the camp's caretaker or owner. If using a private vehicle company to travel to and from the campsite, bring the company's telephone number with you.

Determine the location of the nearest telephone and, if appropriate, post one copy of the emergency telephone numbers next to it. Keep correct change readily available for emergency telephone calls.

Check with the local Girl Scout council for approved sites, special training in handling security and emergencies, and established procedures for particular sites.

Evaluating the Experience

An evaluation is part of every activity and the first step in building future successes. As the leader, you should be evaluating each activity as it is in progress. This allows for changes or adaptations that can improve the total outcome.

Assessing the camping trip with the girls is also essential. The following questions can help them focus on their experience and yield valuable information:

- Was the camping trip fun?
- What part of the trip was most popular, least popular?

- Is there interest in going camping again?
- What should be changed for the next trip?
- What should stay the same?
- What were the new things learned on the camping trip?
- Did you make any new friends because of the camping trip?

Answers to these and other questions can lead to an accurate appraisal of the experience. Comments by parents and guardians also can provide additional information to help evaluate the impact of the experience.

Security, Safety, and Health in the Out-of-Doors

Before going on a camp-out, be familiar with the safety and health guidelines included in this section. Also, it is essential to review *Safety-Wise* for program standards, safety and security guidelines, and activity checkpoints related to camping. Consult this resource to determine the correct ratio of adults to girls for all camping trips.

Security Precautions

Security precautions should be an integral part of the camping experience and should never be regarded lightly. Establish security plans based on general safety precautions and security features of the particular campsite. Keep the following in mind.

Most prowlers prefer to work in the dark and in uninhabited places. They tend to avoid situations where they may be caught, seen, or identified. Effective lighting, locked doors (buildings and cars), the buddy system, noise alarms, and the strategically placed presence of adults become assets that contribute to the security of the group in almost any situation.

If traveling by canoes, bicycles, or other types of easy-to-steal vehicles, take along and *use* chains and locks. Be sure all supplies and equipment are locked up before leaving the campsite.

Have equipment locked in a camp building or monitored by nonparticipating adults while the group is engaged in activities, such as swimming or hiking. Jewelry, large sums of money, and other valuables always should be left at home.

Security procedures differ depending on the location of the campsite and established council methods. Girls should be alerted to these procedures as part of their advance orientation.

With the help of your council, establish some or all of the following precautions as part of a camping security plan.

- Inform law-enforcement officials that your group will be camping in a certain area. Ask officials, in advance, to include your camp in their patrol.
- Check for a perimeter security system such as a fence and a light to define the boundaries of the camp.
- Set up tents within sight of each other. Tents should not be located too close to roads or boundaries.
- Establish an alarm or signal system, which everyone knows, to be used in distress or as a precaution. Practice a code word or whistle, or ring a bell that all campers and adults will recognize. Practice the system at home and upon arrival at the campsite.
- Make the location of all adults on the site known to all campers.
- Develop safety and security procedures for buddy teams to follow if they become separated from the group or get lost.

Finally, establish a few simple rules for all girls to follow:

- Always stay with your buddy. Never walk alone.
- Stay near the group. Don't stray away from the designated camping area.
- Avoid strangers.
- Carry a flashlight at night.
- Report suspicious sounds, activities, or people to an adult in the group.
- Sound an alarm, whistle, or scream when in trouble.
- Move toward people and/or lights when in trouble.

Skits, quiz games, flash card games, and discussions all can be used to alert girls to the safety and security problems that may be encountered at the campsite or en route to the campsite.

The Buddy System

The buddy system is one of the most effective methods of protecting group members while they are engaged in outdoor activities or are away from the regular troop meeting place. The buddy system enables a leader to determine quickly the name of a missing person.

Under the buddy system, the group is divided into teams of two. Each person chooses a buddy and is responsible for: staying with her buddy at all times, warning her buddy of danger, giving her buddy immediate assistance if it is safe to do so, and calling for or going for help when the situation warrants it.

The buddy system does not relieve the leader of her responsibility for knowing the whereabouts of each member of the group, but it does serve as a means of having each person share responsibility. Leaders need to involve everyone in the buddy system during the pretrip planning, at the beginning of each outing, and during the outing. To be really effective, all members of the group need to understand how the buddy system works and how to adapt the buddy system to each separate outing or trip.

Girls and adults can choose their buddies at the start of the trip or upon arrival at the campsite. If there is an odd number, expand one team to include three members. Review all possible hazards, "do's" and "don'ts," the distress code, where adults can be found, where to go for help, etc. During the trip or activity period, leaders or adults in charge should conduct periodic buddy checks.

Staying Found

Everyone should safeguard against the possibility of getting lost. Never set out without telling someone where you are going and when you will be back. If you set out:

- Carry a compass and a map of the area in which you are traveling. Make sure you have learned how to use both correctly.
- Carry rain gear, matches, and extra food and water.
- Be alert and observant at all times so you will be able to find your way back

If, for some reason, you become disoriented and do not know which way to proceed, the best thing to do is to *stop*. Then:

- Sit down and evaluate the circumstances.
- Determine your last known location on the map.
- Orient yourself to the landscape by using the map and compass.
- Listen carefully for noises of traffic, barking dogs, or moving water.
- When you are sure of your location and there is sufficient daylight, plan your trip out of the area and proceed.

If you cannot determine where you are and where you need to go, moving about will not help.

- Sit down, conserve your energy, and relax.
- Find shelter (evergreen grove, rock overhang, a big tree) to keep as warm and dry as possible.
- Devise as many ways as possible to attract the attention of those looking for you: tie a piece of brightly colored cloth to a high branch or rock; flash a mirror or other reflective surface at any passing airplane or helicopter; light a signal fire in a safe, open place (the smoke will call attention to your location); draw large signs on the ground that could be seen from the air.
- Stay in the area. Listen. Make noise if you hear someone nearby.

Natural Disasters

Be prepared for the natural disasters that are most apt to occur in your region of the country. Part of the preparation for each outdoor trip should be a review of the proper response to the emergency situations that can result from lightning, floods, hurricanes, tornadoes, earthquakes, winter storms, or fires. Everyone should practice the procedures for seeking shelter and evacuating a site.

Lightning

Lightning often strikes the tallest object in the area. At the first signs of an impending storm—towering thunderheads, darkening skies, lightning and thunder, and increasing wind—seek shelter.

If available nearby, buildings or automobiles are safe places to seek shelter during the storm. While indoors, stay away from doors, windows, plumbing, and electrical appliances.

If caught outside during a lightning storm:

- Stay away from tall, solitary objects such as trees or electrical poles.
- Avoid standing on a hilltop, exposed ridge, or above the timberline.
- Get out of the water, if swimming.
- Return to land and seek shelter, if in a small boat.
- Avoid touching things made of metal, such as a wire fence.
- Crouch low to the ground in an open area, if sheltered area is not available.

Give prompt first aid to anyone struck by lightning. Do not be afraid to touch or handle the victim; the victim carries no electrical charge. Administer artificial respiration, if necessary, and treat for shock. A victim requiring cardiopulmonary resuscitation (CPR) should be treated only by a trained rescuer. Keep the victim quiet until she has been moved to a hospital.

Winter Storms

Winter storms vary in size and strength and may be blizzards, heavy snowstorms, or ice storms.

When traveling or camping during the winter, ample supplies of food, water, sleeping bags, and blankets should be taken to provide protection if stranded away from shelter. Girls should dress for cold weather in layered, loose-fitting, lightweight clothing.

The following precautions should be taken when caught in a winter storm:

- Listen to a local radio station for storm watch or warning.
- Check battery-powered equipment, emergency cooking facilities, and other emergency gear.
- Seek shelter and avoid traveling during a severe storm.
- Conserve body heat and energy by avoiding overexertion from walking in the snow.
- Use the buddy system when seeking help.
- Know prevention and first aid procedures for hypothermia and frostbite.

Floods and Flash Floods

Floods can occur in almost any part of the United States and usually result from heavy or prolonged rain, rapidly melting snow, or dam breakage. Flash floods can occur with little or no warning and are dangerous because of their swift currents and unpredictable nature. The National Weather Service provides flood alerts. Radio broadcasts provide advance warnings and instructions.

When warnings are provided, evacuate the area swiftly and seek shelter. Extra food and water, flashlights, and dry clothes will be needed. Never camp in dry river beds in areas where an upstream thunderstorm could produce a flash flood.

If evacuation is not possible, determine the best route to high ground. Individuals should not attempt to wade through water higher than knee-deep. Once high ground is reached, wait for rescue parties.

Hurricanes

The following safety rules should be considered before, during, and after a hurricane.

- Listen for warnings on the radio. Have battery-operated radio available in case of power failure.
- Stay away from beaches or other locations that may be swept by tides or storm waves.
- Watch for high water in areas where streams or rivers may flood after heavy rain.
- If in a camp building, board up all windows.
- Store extra food and water.
- Make sure vehicles have gas.
- Seek shelter indoors, away from windows.
- Use the telephone only for emergencies.
- Leave areas such as campsites that might be affected by storm, tide, stream flooding, or falling trees.
- Drive or walk to the nearest designated shelter, using recommended evacuation routes.

- Do not be fooled by the "eye" of the storm (calm period). Winds from the other direction will soon pick up.
- After the storm, stay away from disaster areas. Watch for dangling electrical wires, undermined roads, flooded low spots, or fires. Drive cautiously.

Tornadoes

A tornado is often considered nature's most violent storm because of its destructive force. Darkened skies, thick storm clouds, and strong winds from the south, combined with lightning and periods of rain and hail, often precede a tornado's arrival.

If a tornado warning is issued, take a battery-powered radio and head for a protected area immediately.

Safe places to take shelter include:

- storm shelters and basements
- caves
- tunnels and underground parking facilities
- interior corridors or hallways
- steel-framed or reinforced buildings.

Dangerous places that should be avoided include:

- cars, house trailers, and parked vehicles
- tents
- structures with large, poorly supported roofs
- gymnasiums or auditoriums
- indoors near windows.

If caught outside, move away at right angles to the tornado's path. If there is no time to escape, lie flat in a ditch, ravine, culvert, or under a bridge and protect your head.

Earthquakes

Earthquakes generally threaten areas along faults. The greatest danger of an earthquake is the falling debris.

Keep the following safety rules in mind when faced with an earthquake:

- Keep calm. Don't panic or run.
- If outdoors, get away from buildings, walls, utility poles, or power lines. Head for clear areas.
- If indoors, stand in a doorway or lie under a heavy piece of furniture such as a desk, table, or bed. Stay away from windows. Never run outside; you could be hit by falling debris or live wires.
- After an earthquake, be careful when entering a damaged building.

Fires

Girls should be prepared for fire emergencies. Fire drills should be practiced before the trip and after arrival at the site. When camping in a building, make sure everyone knows how to behave during emergencies, where the exits are, and where to reassemble outside. The paths to the exits should be clear at all times. Everyone should know how to unlock the doors and windows from the inside. (This allows for a quick escape.)

Practice with girls the proper method of extinguishing fire on clothing. Remind the girls to keep calm and roll in the dirt or on the floor. If a blanket or rug is at hand, the girl should wrap herself in the blanket and then roll on the floor or ground.

Review *Safety-Wise* and the *Junior Girl Scout Handbook* for more information on fire safety, and *Cadette and Senior Girl Scout Interest Projects* for activities on Emergency Preparedness.

Some Basics of First Aid

According to the American Red Cross, "first aid is the immediate care given to a person who has been injured or who is suddenly ill." Girl Scouts can be better prepared to prevent accidents and to help when accidents occur if they know first aid and follow safety rules.

The local Girl Scout council or American Red Cross office may provide information on an appropriate first aid course for you and/or the troop to take. It is essential that a trained first aider be on all camping trips. See *Safety-Wise* and check with the local Girl Scout council for safety details.

First Aid Kit

The type and size as well as the contents of the first aid kit will vary according to its use and the size of the group. Consult a physician for specific recommendations. Whether you buy a commercially made first aid kit or the group assembles a kit, it should contain the following items:

adhesive tape and bandages	matches	scissors
Band-Aids, assorted	needle	soap
bottle of distilled water	paper drinking cups	splints
coins for phone calls	petroleum jelly	*Standard First Aid* manual
flashlight	plastic bags for disposal of used materials	table salt
gauze pads		tongue depressors
latex gloves, disposable	roller gauze bandages	triangular bandages
list of emergency phone numbers	safety pins	tweezers

Additional items you may need: sanitary napkins, personal medication with doctor's direction for use attached. Medication should be kept with the leader or camp nurse and given to the girl as directed.

First Aid Emergencies

Some emergencies that may occur in cold or hot weather that girls must be prepared to handle include: hypothermia, frostbite, heatstroke, and heat exhaustion.

Hypothermia

Hypothermia (lowered internal body temperature) occurs when the body loses heat faster than it can produce it. This potentially life-threatening situation can develop when wind, moisture, and cool temperatures draw heat away from the body at a rapid rate. Even when the temperature is far from freezing, a dangerous situation can arise. Because of moisture and wind chill, a cool, breezy, drizzly day can be more dangerous in terms of hypothermia than a calm, dry, cold day. Knowing the following safety procedures for preventing and treating hypothermia can avert an emergency:

Be prepared. Stay warm in cold weather by wearing wool clothing and a hat. The body loses a tremendous amount of heat from the top of the head. Prevent getting wet by covering up or immediately changing wet clothes. Fuel up by eating energy foods and drinking hot drinks.

Know the symptoms. Hypothermia progresses through several stages. Knowing the warning signals can prevent the dangerous progression.
1. Uncontrollable shivering; cold hands and feet.
2. Clumsiness; loss of dexterity.
3. Loss of reason and recall.
4. Shaking; muscular rigidity.
5. Collapse and death.

Treat the victim. Gently warm the victim by administering a warm bath, hot towels or blankets, warm air, or buddy-warming. Seek medical assistance.

The following are hypothermia prevention techniques in water:

HELP (Heat Escape Lessening Position) is assumed to slow cooling from major heat loss areas (groin and sides of chest). In HELP, the most important thing is to keep your head out of the water; then protect the sides of your chest with your arms, cross your ankles to keep your legs together, and, if possible, raise your knees to protect your groin. It's easy to do when sitting on land, but you need to be wearing a Personal Flotation Device to hold the position in water.

Huddle is used to keep several people warm. To huddle, several people hold each other closely, to preserve body heat.

Frostbite

Frostbite, the most common injury caused by exposure to the cold, is the freezing of parts of the body because of exposure to very low temperatures. Frostbite occurs when ice crystals form in the fluid in the cells of skin and tissues. The nose, cheeks, ears, fingers, and toes are most often affected. Recognize the following signs and symptoms of frostbite and learn the appropriate first aid procedures.

Know the symptoms:

1. Skin may be slightly flushed or red.
2. Continued exposure to cold may give skin a gray or white appearance.
3. Pain may be felt early but usually subsides.
4. The affected area feels extremely cold and numb.
5. Often, the victim is not aware she has frostbite until someone notices her symptoms or she observes the pale, glossy skin.

Treat the victim. Protect the frozen area from further injury; warm the frozen area quickly; maintain respiration. Specific first aid procedures include:

- Cover the frozen part with extra clothing or a warm cloth.
- Bring the victim inside promptly.
- Rewarm the frostbitten area rapidly, but gently. Frostbitten tissue is easily damaged, so rubbing of any kind should be avoided. Put the victim's frostbitten part in warm water that is between 39° C (102° F) and 41° C (105° F). Test water temperature with a thermometer or by pouring water over the inside of your arm. Water should feel warm, not hot.
- If warm water is not available, gently wrap the affected part in a sheet and warm blankets.
- Discontinue warming when the part becomes flushed.
- Have the victim exercise the part after it is rewarmed. Raise and lower the affected part to stimulate circulation.
- Clean the frostbitten part with water and mild soap. Rinse thoroughly and blot dry with a sterile cloth.
- If the victim's fingers or toes are involved, place a dry, sterile gauze between them to keep them separated.
- Give fluids such as tea, coffee, or soup if the victim is conscious and not vomiting.
- Obtain medical assistance as soon as possible.

- Do not rub the frozen part, break blisters, or allow the victim to sit near a radiator, stove, or fire. Do not use heat lamps, hot water bottles, electric blankets, or heating pads. If feet are affected, do not allow the victim to walk.

Heatstroke

Heatstroke, a disturbance in the body's regulating system, is caused by extremely high body temperature due to exposure to heat. Heatstroke is a life-threatening emergency; therefore, you must be prepared to act quickly to reduce the victim's body temperature at once. Knowing the following symptoms and first aid procedures will help girls be prepared to act quickly.

Know the symptoms:

1. Body temperature is extremely high, often 41° C (106° F) or higher.
2. Skin is hot, red, and dry.
3. Pulse is rapid and strong.
4. Victim may be unconscious.

Treat the victim. If the victim's body temperature reaches 40° C (105° F):

- Undress the victim and sponge bare skin continuously with cool water or rubbing alcohol; or apply cold packs continuously; or place the victim in a tub of cold water (not iced). Continue treatment until body temperature is lowered; then dry the victim. (The victim also may be cooled off with a fan or air conditioner, if available.) If body temperature rises again, repeat cooling process.
- Do not give the victim alcoholic beverages or stimulants such as coffee or tea.
- Seek medical assistance.

Heat Exhaustion

Heat exhaustion can occur after prolonged exposure to high temperatures and high humidity, and is the result of inadequate intake of water to compensate for loss of fluids through sweating.

Know the symptoms:

1. Body temperature is normal or near normal.
2. Skin becomes white or pale and cool and clammy.
3. Weakness, nausea, and dizziness can occur.
4. Cramps or fainting may take place.

Treat the victim:

- Move the victim to a cool, shaded area.
- Give the victim sips of salt water—made by adding 5 milliliters (one teaspoon) of salt per glass. The victim may drink half a glass every 15 minutes for one hour. Stop fluids if vomiting occurs.
- Lay victim down and raise her feet from 20 to 30 centimeters (8 to 12 inches).
- Loosen clothing and apply cool, wet cloths on the victim's forehead and body.
- Fan the victim or move her to an air-conditioned room.
- If symptoms worsen, become severe, or last longer than an hour, seek medical attention promptly.

Water Safety

Follow the procedures in *Safety-Wise* when swimming or using a small craft. In addition, check any local, state, or federal regulations that might be in effect regarding water safety. Water safety training is available from several sources including the YMCA and the American Red Cross.

Water Supply

Before going camping, check on the available water supply at the site. Only water from a tap tested by the local health department can be considered safe to use. All other sources of water such as lakes, streams, or ponds must be purified. Even sparkling clear water can be contaminated by chemicals, dead animals, or unsanitary conditions upstream out of view. Drinking unpurified water can lead to diarrhea and a host of gastrointestinal diseases. Several water purification methods are available and you should check with the local Girl Scout council to see which method is preferred by local health officials. Also check for water purification methods in *Safety-Wise*.

Water Purification Methods

If the water is not clear and clean-looking, the first step in purifying water is to pour it through a clean cloth to filter out solid particles and organic matter. Then use one of the methods below:

Commercial water purification kit—These portable water filters range in price from $30 to $295. Instructions for use are included with the filter.

Water purification tablets—Water purification tablets have a short shelf life so be sure to look at the expiration date before using. In general, the higher the water temperature and the longer the chemicals (in the tablet) are dissolved in the water, the better the chances are of killing harmful organisms. Be sure to follow instructions on the package.

Liquid chlorine bleach—Usually has 2 to 6 percent available chlorine. Read the label to find the percentage of chlorine in the solution; then follow this treatment for each liter (quart) of water:

Percentage of Chlorine in Solution	Drops of Bleach Added to Each Liter of Water (Clean Water)*	Drops of Bleach Added to Each Quart of Water (Clean Water)
1	25	20
4-6	5	4
7-10	3	2
If not known	5	4

*Double number of drops for cloudy, cold water. Shake and then let stand for 30 minutes.

Boiling—Water maintained at a rapid boil for one minute at sea level should be safe to drink. This will eliminate bacteria but not viruses or chemical contaminants. At 3,048 meters (10,000 feet), water must be boiled for five minutes to have the same effect. An additional purification method may be needed to make the water completely safe.

Once water has been purified, it should be stored in a clean, covered container.

The protozoan *Giardia lamblia* is of increasing concern to backcountry campers. If present in the water source, only boiling the water or pouring it through specially designed filters will remove the *Giardia* organism. Ingestion of *Giardia* can cause diarrhea, loss of appetite, dehydration, and cramps.

Personal Hygiene

Good health habits are particularly important when camping. Girls should be reminded to practice the same good grooming habits at camp that they practice at home: brush teeth after meals, wash hands and face, and shower.

If bathrooms or latrines are provided at the site, girls should clean them daily as part of their kapers (unless a cleaning service is provided at the site). Paper supplies should be replenished, the floor swept, and toilets and sinks cleaned. Toilet seats should be cleaned with a disinfectant solution.

If a toilet or a latrine is not available, dig a hole one-half meter (18 inches) deep in a private place. The soil removed from the hole should be piled at the side so that each time the toilet is used some earth is scattered into the hole.

At remote, short-term use sites, each person can make a "cat" hole by scraping away the upper layer of soil with her heel. Cover the waste with soil. Used toilet paper should be carried out in a plastic bag and disposed of properly. Practicing proper disposal of human wastes will help keep water sources pure.

Handwashing

If running tap water is not available, a simple handwashing unit can be made from a plastic jug and a wooden dowel or twig. Make a small hole near the bottom of the jug. Use the twig or dowel to plug up the hole once you've filled the jug with water. Place a bar of biodegradable soap in an old stocking and tie this to the handle of the jug. Now hang one of these handwashing units near the latrine and the kitchen. For better water flow, remove the cap from the jug.

Hint: Remove a bar of soap from its package and let it dry for several days before the trip. This will cause the bar to lose excess moisture and harden. The soap will last longer.

Showers

If ready-made showers are not available on the trip, an improvised shower can be constructed. Remember to include daily cleaning of showers on your kaper chart.

The most common improvised shower is a bucket (painted black to absorb heat) suspended on a tree or pole with a pull cord attached to the top. Pull on the cord to tip the bucket, allowing just enough water to get wet all over. Soap yourself using biodegradable soap, then tip the bucket again for a quick but thorough rinse. In addition to this method, many commercial portable showers are now available.

Clothes Washing

When a camping trip of several days or weeks is planned, you'll need to think about washing clothes before they become too heavily soiled. Frequent washing prevents soils and stains from setting and promotes a cleaner, healthier environment. When clothes washing is necessary, consider the following.

- Warm water to wash clothes by letting buckets stand in the sun.
- Make an improvised washing machine by shaking dirty socks and underwear in a tightly covered can half-filled with soapy water.
- Set up a clothes-washing production line with three buckets: one each for wash, rough rinse, and final rinse.
- Wet dirty clothes, rub soiled spots with soap, and work up and down in a pail of water.
- Use cake soap rather than detergent for rubbing soiled clothes.

Dishwashing

Dishwashing is easier if dishes aren't too dirty. Scrape plates or wipe with a paper napkin and presoak pots before washing.

Dishwashing for a group works most efficiently with a little preplanning.

- To make pots easy to clean, rub soap over the bottom and sides of the *outside* of the pot before the pot is placed on the fire. A bar of soap or liquid dishwashing soap can be used.

- Heat dish water on your cooking fire soon after the fire is lit so it will be ready when the meal is finished. In addition to saving time, you will be saving fuel.
- Soak dirty pots and utensils while eating.

Use three buckets or deep pans for dishwashing. The first bucket contains hot, soapy water; the second bucket contains clean water for rinse; and the third contains boiling water or a sanitizing solution for sterilization. Keep dish water clean by washing least dirty items such as cups and silverware first, and pots last. Sanitize dishes by rinsing in clear boiling water for one minute or immersing them in a sanitizing solution approved by the local health department.

Individual net bags hold dishes during the final sterilizing rinse in boiling water. They are then hung up to air dry. When dry, dishes and eating utensils, still in bags, are stored away from dust.

Used dish water should be filtered to remove any food particles and then scattered, not poured, on the ground. Scatter the water away from the main campsite and at least 60 meters (200 feet) from any natural water source. In many camps, there will be a waste water dumpsite. Remember, dirty water drained into a water supply can create a serious health hazard. Filtered food particles should be added to the garbage.

Garbage Disposal

Camp garbage disposal calls for advance planning. Inquire ahead about local regulations and facilities. If a garbage pickup service is available, line cans with plastic bags and make sure they are tightly covered at all times. Sort out those items that can be recycled. Otherwise, carry out all garbage. Flatten cans to save space when carrying out. Papers may be burned where permitted.

Living in the Out-of-Doors

Tents

Choosing the Right Tent
If tent camping is decided upon, you will need to consider the type of tents to use. Tents should be chosen to suit the shelter

needs of the troop and should provide protection from rain, snow, sun, wind, insects, and snakes.

Check with the local Girl Scout council as well as troop members and their families as you investigate tent needs. Consider the following questions during planning:

- How many girls are going on the trip?
- How will equipment be transported?
- What type of tents are available?
- What type of weather is expected?
- What facilities are at the campsite?

Other important features of the tent to consider are:

- flame resistance
- weight
- ventilation
- insectproof design
- waterproof material and design
- head room
- floor
- fabric (breathes and allows air flow)
- ease of assembly
- portability.

Today, most tents are made of lightweight, fire-retardant materials, but no tent is fireproof. Never place a candle, camp stove, lantern, or open flame in a tent. Pitch tents far enough from the cooking fire so that the wind cannot blow a spark onto the tent. Never use plastic as a sleeping shelter.

Setting Up the Campsite

If you are camping at a well-established campsite, cooking and tent sites may already be designated. These should be used in order to minimize the impact of camping activities on the rest of the site.

If you are camping in an area where sites are not designated, the following points should be considered.

- Groups of 10 people or less have significantly less adverse impact on the site. Ten is the maximum group size in some parks and national forests.

- Avoid camping in fragile areas—i.e., areas with wet soil; above the timberline; on the tundra; or in mountain meadows.

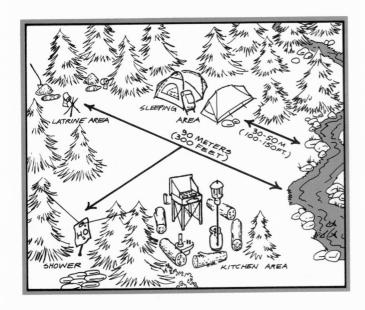

- Choose level ground that is 30 to 50 meters (100 to 150 feet) from the water source or the trail.

- If there are several drinking water sources to choose from, choose fast-moving water rather than still or stagnant water. Springs and snow offer other possible water sources for drinking. (See page 29 on water purification.)

- Decide which areas will be used for tents, food preparation, and toilets.

- Fires and stoves should be built or placed 3 meters (10 feet) or more downwind from tents.

- Determine the direction of storm fronts and good weather fronts. Pitch tents for protection from storms by using the natural shelter provided by hills, vegetation, etc.

- In summer, choose a site that will get sun in the morning and shade in the afternoon.

- Avoid dry creek beds, which are susceptible to flash floods.

- Choose a site clear of any dead overhanging branches. Do not pitch a tent under any branch that might fall if the wind increases.

- Areas with pine needles or dead leaves provide an extra mattress for sleeping. Do not remove this ground cover.

- Set up a cooking area that is sheltered from the wind and that has no overhanging branches. If a cooking fire is necessary, build it in an area with mineral soil.

- If mosquitoes or flies present a problem, try to choose a site away from water. A breeze will help blow away flying insects.

- Special precautions should be taken to protect food from ants, chipmunks, raccoons, mice, skunks, porcupines, and bears. Hanging all food and garbage from a tree limb at night will help keep unwanted visitors from consuming your food supply. If you plan to camp in an area where there are bears, check with local authorities for special instructions about hanging food. Food should not be kept in sleeping tents!

Pitching the Tent

Pitching the tent will be a manageable task at the campsite if the troop has practiced pitching the tent several times before the trip. Someone familiar with setting up the type of tent the troop is using could provide a valuable demonstration. Mark corresponding tent poles with tape to make setup easier. Before unrolling the tent, carefully choose the tent site. Although tents usually come with instructions for pitching, below are some important particulars to remember.

- Pitch the tent on level ground, at least 30 to 50 meters (100 to 150 feet) away from water sources. Be sure that the tent is not pitched in an area that may be suddenly under water—for example, in a flood plain, a dry river bed, or a ditch near a steep slope. Drive tent pegs into the ground at a 90° angle to the guy rope.

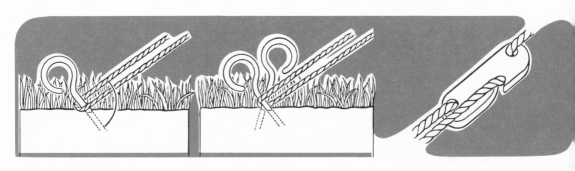

- When pitching a tent in snow, stamp down the snow in the pitching site and use snow pegs or snow anchors to secure the tent.

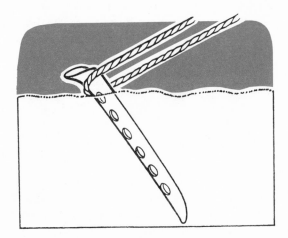

- Determine the general direction of prevailing winds. In stormy or cold weather, the tent should be pitched so the open end faces away from the wind. In hot weather, pitch the tent so the opening catches the breeze.

- Avoid pitching the tent under dead trees. Dead tree limbs may fall on the tent.

- Make every effort not to disturb the environment. Do not uproot large rocks or logs. Do not dig holes or trenches. Leave the site without a trace of it having been used.

- Remove any loose stones, twigs, or branches from the ground but leave pine needles and dead leaves as these provide an extra cushion for sleeping.

Caring for the Tent

Proper care of the tent will add to its longevity and demonstrate the troop's responsibility and respect for property.

Seal tent seams at least once a year. Follow the directions on the seam sealer, which can be obtained at a local sporting goods or hardware store. Commercial waterproofing agents can be applied to the entire tent but be sure to follow the directions carefully.

Materials to repair holes or rips in tents as well as spare parts should be carried on all trips. Items include needle and nylon thread, special tapes, or self-adhesive fabrics. Spare parts include tent pegs, guy rope, and poles.

To secure a tent in case of high winds, storm lashing may be used. Storm lashing helps prevent a tent from flapping, ripping, or being knocked down. Use two lengths of 6-millimeter (one-quarter inch) rope. Run one rope from its own heavy-duty peg at A to and around the tent pole spike at B and back to peg C. Use the other rope in the reverse direction to form the double X shown.

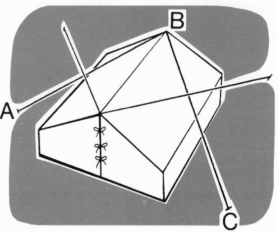

When repacking, do not roll up a wet or damp tent, if possible. If you must, remember to hang up the tent later to dry. Brush off the tent when rolling it up. Clean off stakes and place them in a separate bag. Be sure to store a dry tent in a waterproof sack.

Knots

Knots are used for a variety of camp needs, such as setting up your tent and securing canoes or boats. Knowing how to tie knots and what each knot is used for is important. There are more than 8,000 different knots to tie!

It is important to know the basic parts of the rope: the free end or working end, the bight (the bend in the rope), and the standing end.

Knots are made of three simple turns:

To prevent the ends of a rope from fraying, the rope is whipped or stopped.

To whip a rope, a piece of string 20 to 30 centimeters (8 to 12 inches) long is needed. Make a loop at one end of the string and lay the loop along the rope with the ends of the string hanging off the end of the rope.

Use your finger to hold this loop of string in place. Wind the long end of the string tightly over the loop and around the rope. The short end of the string will be left hanging. Wind the string around the rope for about 2 centimeters (one inch). Generally, the length of your whipping should be about the same as the diameter of the rope. Wind tightly but do not overlap. Tuck the end of the string you have been winding through the loop. Hold it with your thumb so it will not loosen.

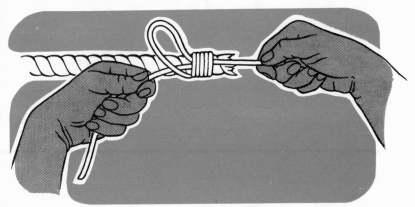

Pull slowly on the other end of the string. The loop will disappear under the winding. Pull until the loop is halfway under the winding. Trim off the ends to make a neat whipping.

Overhand Knot

The overhand knot is useful for tying cord around a pin to end a macramé project, holding beads in place, and tying your shoes! It also makes a nice variety knot in a macramé design.

1. Make a loop and bring one end around the rope and through the loop.

2. Pull the ends of the rope tightly.

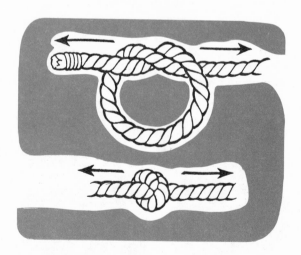

Square Knot

The square knot is used to join two ropes of the same thickness. The square knot also is used to tie a bandage in place. To make a square knot, use two pieces of rope or both ends of your knotting rope. (A knotting rope is a rope used to practice making knots.)

1. Hold one end of the rope in each hand. Cross end A over end B, then push it under and up behind.

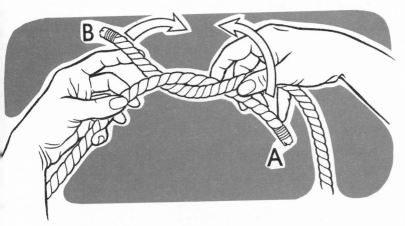

2. Then cross A over B end again, pushing A around and under B and up through the loop.

3. Tighten by pulling both loose ends.

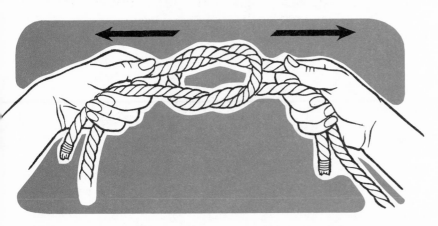

Half Hitch

The half hitch is a simple turn used to fasten the end of a rope after it has been looped around something, such as a bedroll or post, or through a ring.

1. Loop the end of the rope around the post or through the ring.

2. Make a half hitch by looping the short end of the rope under the long end and through the space created.

3. Make a second half hitch below the first half hitch, and you have two half hitches. Two half hitches make a sliding knot that moves along the standing part of the rope. The sliding knot is used to change the tension on the rope without retying the knot each time.

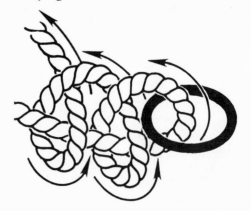

Clove Hitch

The clove hitch is used to fasten one end of a rope around a post or a tree; for instance, the clove hitch is used when putting up a clothesline between two trees. If kept taut, the knot will not slip.

1. Pass the short end of the rope around the back of the post or tree.

2. Bring the short end around in front and cross it over the long part of the rope, making an "X."

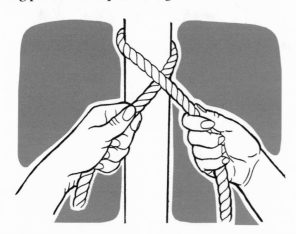

3. Hold the "X" with your thumb and forefinger while you wrap the rope around the post again below the first turn.

4. Push the rope end under the "X," so that the end comes out between the two turns around the post.

5. Pull the short end with one hand and the long end with the other. As long as there is a steady pull on the long end, the hitch will not loosen.

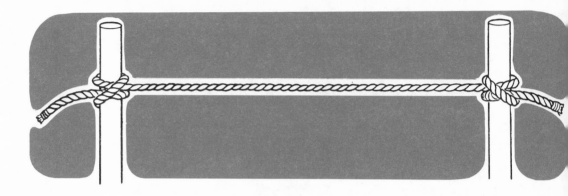

Taut-line Hitch
The taut-line hitch is used to make a loop that is adjustable in length. The hitch slides along the standing part of the rope and is useful in adjusting the tension on tent ropes.

1. Loop the short end of the rope around the tent peg.

2. Wind the short end of the rope around the standing part twice.

3. Fasten the short end to the standing part with a half hitch above the previous loops.

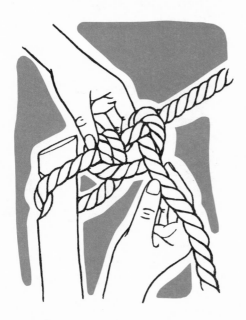

4. The tension of the length of the rope can be easily adjusted by sliding the knot back and forth along the rope.

Sheet Bend

The sheet bend is used to tie two ropes of different thicknesses together. It's really a square knot with an extra twist to make it hold tightly.

1. Make a square knot.

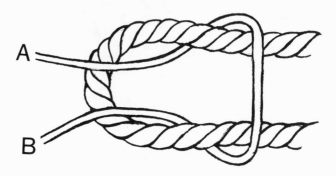

2. Cross the short end of the thinner rope (A) over the long end and tuck it down through the longer loop of the thicker rope.

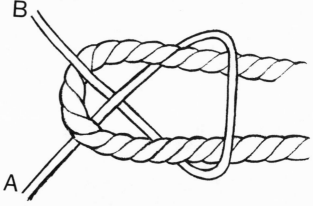

3. Pull the knot tightly. This extra turn will hold the small end in place.

Sheepshank

The sheepshank is used to shorten a rope without cutting it. You can shorten a rope with a sheepshank as long as both ends of the rope create tension throughout the length of the rope.

1. Fold the loose part of the rope you wish to tighten into the shape of an "S."

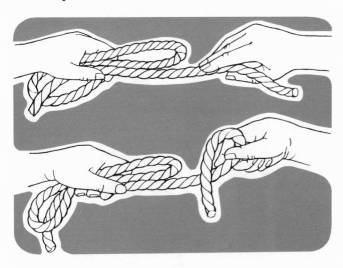

2. By twisting the standing part of the rope, tie a half hitch around each end of the loops.

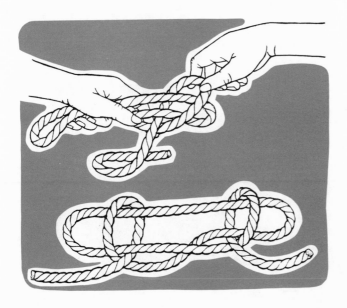

Bowline

The bowline is used at the end of a rope to form a loop that will remain the same size. The knot can be used to form a loop over a peg or hook or to make a loop around a post, a tree, or your waist.

1. Make a small loop by passing the working end over the standing end of the rope. (The length of the rope from this loop to the end of the working portion of the rope will be the approximate circumference of the final loop that will be formed.)

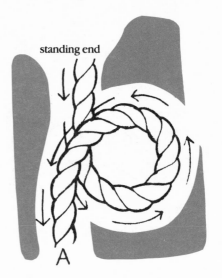

2. Bring end A up through the loop.

3. Pass end A beneath the standing part of the rope.

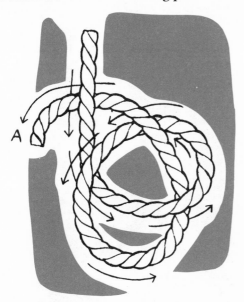

4. Push end A through the loop again.

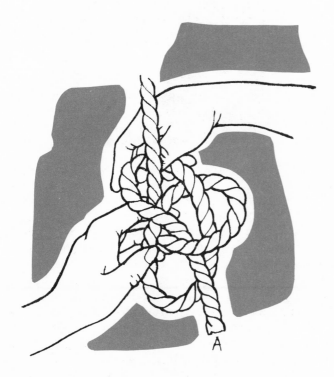

5. Tighten by pulling on the standing and working ends of the rope.

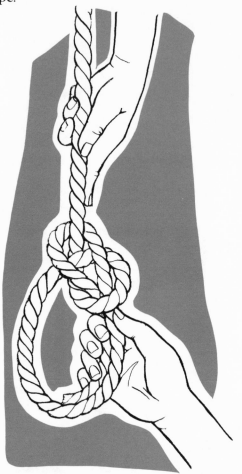

An easy way to teach this knot is to tell a story to go with it.

In the ancient land of the "sixes" lives a princess who likes to sit at the edge of a lake and watch the reflections. (Form a small "six" in the rope by looping the working end over a portion of the standing portion of the rope. The lake is represented by the loop just formed. The princess is represented by the standing part of the rope.) One day as the princess sits by the lake, a dragon with a long body rises from the lake. (Push the working end of the rope up through the loop.) The dragon slithers around the princess and heads back into the lake. (Pass the working end beneath the standing part of the rope and push it down through the loop again.) The princess cries "help" and you can rescue her by grasping the princess with one hand and the dragon's head and tail with your other hand. Now pull!

Knives

Along with the privilege of having a knife comes the responsibility of using it properly to ensure the safety of users, other campers, and the environment. Troop members need to learn how to use knives safely and how to take care of, maintain, and store them in good condition.

A jackknife is a knife with a folding blade that will be used often for a wide variety of tasks: cutting a rope, scraping a carrot, trimming a branch, or whittling a toggle.

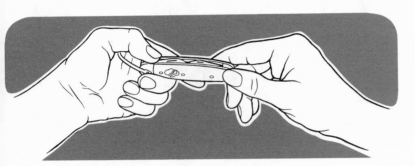

Jackknives sometimes have more than one blade or tool. The knife may include an awl for drilling holes, a can opener, or a combination screwdriver and bottle-cap opener. For safety, only one tool should be opened at a time.

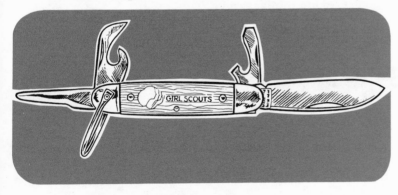

Some tips for using the jackknife are:

- Hold the handle securely with the whole hand.
- Always cut away from the body.
- Move at least an arm's length away from anyone else before using a knife.
- Keep the knife closed when not in use.
- Do not walk around with an open knife.
- Keep the knife away from extreme cold or heat.

Opening the Jackknife

Hold the jackknife firmly with the fingers of one hand. Hold the top edge (slot) of the blade with your thumb and forefinger.

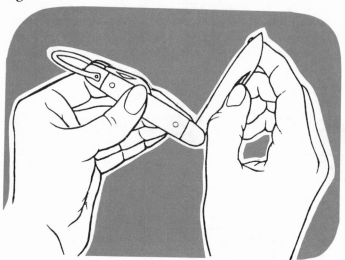

Keep your fingers away from the sharp cutting edge of the blade. Pull the blade all the way out until it clicks into its open position.

Closing the Jackknife

Hold the handle of the jackknife in one hand with the sharp cutting side of the blade upward.

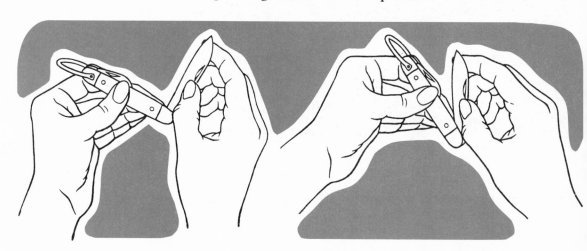

Hold the dull, noncutting side of the blade in the other hand. Push the blade up and around toward the slot in the handle.

Whittling a Point

Whittle a point with the jackknife to make tent stakes, poles, skewers for cooking, etc. To whittle correctly:

- Hold the handle of the jackknife firmly. Do not put your thumb on the blade.
- Cut away from the body.
- Cut slowly so the knife won't slip.
- Cut the stick at an angle from thicker end to thinner end.
- Shape the stick by cutting off little pieces of wood. Do not try to cut off big pieces.

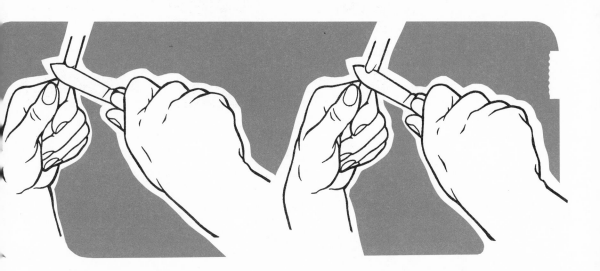

Passing the Knife

Always close a jackknife before you pass it. When handling other knives, grasp the knife blade along the dull edge and pass the handle to the other person. This way, you have control of the sharp edge of the knife.

When not in use, a jackknife should be kept closed and in a pocket. A lanyard or sinnet of macramé could be made as a holder to hang from a belt or pack.

Sharpening the Knife

A sharp knife is safer than a dull knife. Be sure to include a sharpening stone on your list of items to bring.

The sharpening stone should be lubricated with oil or water before using. Use the stone's coarse grit first to remove nicks, then follow with the medium grit and, finally, the fine grit to hone the edge to perfection.

Hold the stone in one hand and the open knife in the other. Keep the fingers holding the stone below the top edge of the sharpening stone.

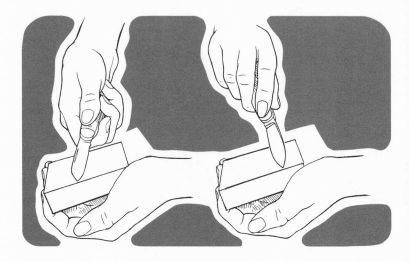

Lay the flat side of the knife blade on the flat surface of the stone. The knife will be at a slight (15° - 20°) angle to the stone, with the unsharpened edge of the blade slightly raised.

Keeping this angle, move the blade across the stone in a slicing motion, following a semi-circular path, pivoting the blade toward the point. Make sure the total edge of the blade is in contact with the stone.

Turn the knife over and start again at the base of the blade, repeating the slicing motion, but in the opposite direction. The knife blade and the sharpening stone may become warm from the friction.

Test the sharpness of the knife by cutting a piece of wood or a piece of rope.

Cleaning the Jackknife

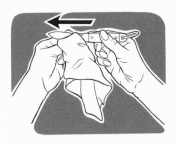

- Always keep the knife clean and dry.
- Hold the cleaning cloth at the back of the blade away from the cutting edge.
- Wipe the blade clean and dry as you draw the cloth toward the blade's tip.
- Wipe carefully across the whole blade.
- Oil the jackknife's hinge with machine oil.
- Never clean the blade by rubbing it in dirt or sand.

Cooking in the Out-of-Doors

Wood Fires

In the past, wood fires had been the primary source of heat for cooking for many campers. As a result of gathering wood, building fire circles, and building fires too close to rocks and trees, heavily used camping areas have been severely impacted. In many national parks and forests, campfires are now prohibited or restricted. Today, Girl Scouts are encouraged to use charcoal and portable stoves instead of wood.

Wood fires, however, may be used for cooking where wood is plentiful or in emergencies for warmth or signaling. The choice of fuel will depend upon availability, environmental impact, cost, safety, and the kind of cooking to be done.

The three basic elements for a fire are fuel, flame (or intense heat), and air (oxygen). To build a wood fire, different sizes of wood—tinder, kindling, and fuel—will be needed and should be assembled in a manner that will allow for circulation of air.

Tinder is any small piece of material that burns as soon as it is touched with a match. Tinder can be dry wood, dried leaves, or wood shavings.

Other materials for tinder could be dried pine needles or cones, bark from a dead tree, or paper twisted into spirals.

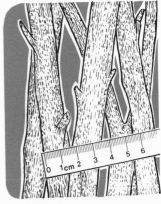

Kindling is larger in diameter than tinder. Kindling must be thin enough to catch fire quickly before the tinder burns out, but large enough to ignite the larger fuel.

Twigs or splintered pieces of wood can be used for kindling. Both tinder and kindling should be as dry as possible to catch fire quickly. To test dryness, see if wood snaps, not bends, when broken.

Fuel is the larger wood that keeps a fire going. Fuel might be charcoal or dry, seasoned wood found on the ground. At some sites, it may be necessary to bring fuel with you.

When building a fire, consider the type of wood you are using. Hardwoods, such as oak, hickory, birch, maple, ash, eucalyptus, and mesquite, produce a long-burning fire with lasting coals. Softwoods, such as pine, spruce, cedar, gray birch, or aspen, produce a quick, hot fire and provide excellent fuel for starting a long-burning fire with harder wood.

Starting the Fire

Fire starters are highly flammable materials that ignite at the touch of a match. The simplest fire starters are stubs of candles, twists of a paper napkin or newspaper, or strips of milk cartons.

The troop may want to make fire starters as part of their preparation activities before the trip. Two types of fire starters that can be made before a camping trip include "egg" fire starters and trench candles.

"EGG" FIRE STARTERS (WAXED EGG CARTON)

1. Fill cardboard egg cartons half-full of sawdust, lint, or wood shavings.

2. Pour melted paraffin or candle ends into each compartment until each space is full. (Wax should be melted in a double boiler and poured with adult supervision.)

3. When cool, break apart each "egg" or store the whole carton for future use.

4. Place one "egg" in the kindling and light a match.

TRENCH CANDLES

1. Roll several sheets of newspaper into a long, tight roll.

2. Tie the roll with string at 6-centimeter (about 2¹/₂-inch) intervals. Leave an 8-centimeter (about 3-inch) end on each string for dipping. Cut the roll between the strings.

3. Dip each trench candle into a container of melted wax.

4. Hang by the strings to dry.

Building the Fire

Before building any fire:

- Consider the environment. Are there air pollution regulations?

- Check local fire ordinances. Will a fire destroy the ground cover or the natural beauty of the land, or leave a scar?

- Check local weather conditions. Is it too dry or windy for a safe fire?

- Choose a spot away from trails or traffic patterns.

- Choose a spot with no overhanging tree limbs, rock ledges, rotting stumps, logs, grass, or leaves.

- Always have a large bucket of water or sand near the fire before striking the first match.

- Tie back long hair, roll up loose sleeves, and do not wear clothing with dangling ends while building or tending a fire. Plastic or synthetic garments are extremely flammable and can cause severe burns as they often melt rather than burn. Natural fibers are much safer.

- With wood or charcoal, plan a fire just big enough to do the job so fuel will not be wasted. Would several small fires be better and safer? How about a long narrow fire to heat a row of pots?

- Make sure there is enough dead wood to sustain a fire.

- If you build a fire on the ground, clear the ground to bare earth or rock with no roots underneath. A circle of one meter (3 to 4 feet) in diameter must be cleared. In areas of peat soil, duff, or a deep layer of pine needles, you may need to build the fire in a fireplace or off the ground on a cement slab or piece of tin.

- Use a ready-made fireplace or improvise a raised fireplace using a wheelbarrow, large can, or charcoal stove in areas where underground fire danger is great. (Remember to protect the environment.)

Once you have considered the precautions outlined above, follow these four steps to build a fire:

1. Make a small triangle with three pieces of kindling.

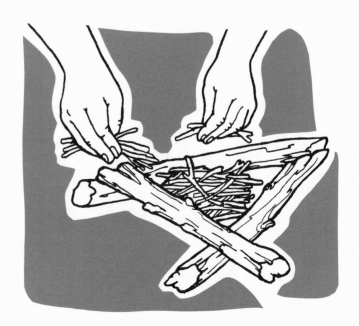

2. Leave an air space under the top bar of the triangle. Lay a handful of tinder upright against the top stick. (A fire starter may be used in place of tinder.)

3. Strike the match close to the wood. Hold the match beneath the tinder until the flame burns up through the tinder. Then place additional tinder and kindling onto the fire. Place each piece of kindling separately. Remember to have enough extra tinder, kindling, and fuel within close reach.

4. Fires need oxygen to burn. Arrange the wood so that a small space lies between each piece. Place the pieces of wood close enough so one piece of burning wood will light the adjoining pieces. Once the kindling is burning, add fuel. Fuel may be wood or charcoal. Use just enough fuel for your cooking needs.

If you need to concentrate the heat of the fire under a pot to heat water, for example, continue to add pieces of kindling to form a cone. If you need to cook food for a longer period of time, add more kindling and then fuel to the fire. As the fuel burns down, the bed of coals formed will provide a more even, long-lasting heat source.

When finished cooking with any type of wood fire:

• Let the fire die down until only ashes are left.

• Stir the ashes, sprinkle them with water, then stir them again. Repeat until there is no gray ash anywhere in the fire bowl. Do not pour water on a fireplace. The water may cause the stones to crack.

- A hand passed several inches above the ashes will indicate whether or not the spot is still hot. Then hold a steady hand several inches above the ashes.

- Finally, when a hand can be pressed and not feel any warmth on the spot where the fire was, the fire is out.

- Cover the fire circle with rocks, dirt, or sand when cleaning up at the end of the trip. Return the area to its natural condition.

Charcoal Fires

Charcoal, like other fuels, needs air to burn. A ready-made charcoal stove in a park or backyard has been designed to enhance air flow. If you are making your own charcoal stove, construct it so that a draft of air flows past the charcoal. A charcoal stove for one person can be made from a large tin can.

Tin Can Charcoal Stove

You need:
Tin can, #10 or larger   2 pieces of sturdy wire
Roll-type can opener   screen
Soda can opener   3 to 4 charcoal briquettes
Wire for handle

1. Remove top of can with roll-type can opener. Punch air-holes with soda can opener around top and bottom of can. The bottom holes are the openings through which the stove should be lit.

2. Push ends of wire through two of the holes at top and twist to make a handle. This handle is convenient when it's time to pack up, but beware of the hot handle while cooking.

3. Push wire screen halfway down into can to make a grate. This holds charcoal near the top for cooking and provides air space under charcoal.

HANDLE

4. Make a stove top out of the second piece of wire screen. This supports the pot.

Set the stove on cleared ground and put tinder or fire starters on the grate. Carefully pile charcoal to allow proper air flow. It takes half an hour for a charcoal fire to reach the "ember stage" (gray coals) for cooking.

Extinguishing a Charcoal Fire
Charcoal must be well soaked with water before you can consider it extinguished. When the cooking is done, carefully sprinkle water over each piece of charcoal. Lay the charcoal out to dry for reuse.

Put the charcoal in a tin can with a tight cover and take it with you. If not taking the charcoal with you, make sure to crush each piece of charcoal with a rock to ensure that the coals are completely extinguished.

Stoves

Selection
When selecting a stove, consider design. The more "yes" answers to the following questions, the more desirable the stove.

- Is the stove base wider than the pot support surface? Does the stove (with the pot on it) have a low center of gravity, so it is not easily tipped over?
- Is the stove free from sharp or protruding edges?
- Is the stove's cooking capacity large enough for the number of people in the group?
- Is the stove strong enough to take rough handling?
- Is the stove designed for easy assembly, with a minimum of moving or connecting parts and welded surfaces?
- Is the stove designed for easy cleaning?
- Will the stove start without priming?
- Is there air space between flame and pot when the flame is high?
- Does the fuel tank stay cool when the stove is lit?
- Will the stove function above 1,800 meters (6,000 feet)? (Answer if the stove is to be used at high altitudes.)
- Will the stove function in below-freezing temperatures? (Answer if the stove is to be used in sub-freezing temperatures.)

Fuel

Stoves that use fuels listed below are recommended; however, these fuels warrant safety precautions because they are potentially dangerous. Be sure to follow the operating instructions that come with each stove.

Propane: Some of the safest and most efficient stoves burn propane. This fuel comes in pressurized tanks and is available in most sporting goods stores. A one-pound tank will burn four to six hours. Refueling is easy, a matter of replacing the tank. Propane is dependable at high altitudes and in freezing temperatures. Propane tanks are heavier than butane tanks.

Butane: Butane also comes in pressurized tanks. The stove is refueled by replacing the tank. It is clean and easily operated. Excellent at above-freezing temperatures, it does not function well when the temperature dips below freezing. Butane loses some of its efficiency when the fuel supply in the tank gets low. Cooking time with butane is longer than with kerosene.

Kerosene: The kerosene stove can be set directly on snow or on a cold surface and still operate efficiently. Kerosene costs only a few pennies per hour to burn. However, kerosene is heavy, smokes, smells, and is difficult to start. It does not evaporate quickly and leaves a residue wherever spilled.

Ethyl Alcohol: Alcohol burns at low temperatures, producing only half as much heat as kerosene. Since it is not a petroleum product, an alcohol fire can be put out with water. It is more expensive to use than kerosene.

Sterno: Sterno is safer than liquid fuels and relatively inexpensive, but has low heating power. More sterno is required to cook a meal than with other types of fuel.

Remember: If a fuel container is used and emptied on the trip, carry it out for proper disposal. Never put an empty fuel container in a fire.

Efficiency

The following factors influence stove efficiency:

Altitude. The higher the altitude, the longer the cooking time. It takes twice as long to boil an egg at 3,000 meters (about 9,500 feet) than at sea level.

Pot lid. Food cooks faster in a covered pot.

Amount of fuel. A full tank works more efficiently than a tank that is almost empty.

Oxygen. Lack of oxygen and reduced air pressure reduce fuel performance.

Temperature. Below-freezing temperatures reduce efficiency.

Wind. Wind cools fuel and the cooking pot and blows the flame away from the pot, thus increasing cooking time.

Type of food. "Add hot water" foods are faster to prepare than "simmer an hour" foods. Large pieces of food take longer to cook than smaller pieces.

Distance of flame to pot. The closer the flame to the pot, the faster the food will cook.

Size of flame. The size of the flame should match the size of the pot.

Heat of flame. The hotter the flame, the more rapidly food will cook. A flame appears blue to white when it is hottest and red when it is coolest.

Safety
Always read and follow stove instructions carefully before operating. The following safety precautions should be taken.

• Test the stove and become familiar with its operation before taking it camping.

• All persons on a camping trip should know about the operation of the stove. Anyone operating the stove should have been trained to use the stove properly and safely. A trained adult should be present to supervise the use of any stove.

• Practice replacing parts before taking the stove on a camping trip—know the proper tools to use.

- When replacing parts of a stove, make sure the parts are correct and approved by the manufacturer.

- Keep all stove parts clean and see that lines and burners are not clogged. Make sure all rubber or plastic lines are not cracked or cut. Maintain the stove according to the manufacturer's instructions.

- Always store fuel away from the stove and other heat sources. Use containers designed and marked for fuel.

- When a key is used to regulate the flow of fuel to the burner, be sure to remove it when not in use; it can become too hot to handle.

- Keep combustible materials including sleeping bags and clothes away from stoves and fuel. Never use a stove inside a tent.

- When refueling, be sure the stove is on a level surface and away from an open flame. If fuel spills, relocate the stove before lighting.

- Always let a stove cool before refueling with liquid fuels.

- When using liquid fuels, use a funnel to transfer the fuel from the container to the stove.

- To avoid flare-up when lighting the stove, do not overfill.

- For stoves that require priming, be careful to avoid over-priming and spilling fuel.

- When replacing pressure tanks, be certain all connections are tight, with no leakage.

- If the stove has a refillable tank, before each meal make sure the tank has enough fuel to cook the meal.

- Never use pots that make the stove top-heavy. Always make certain that the cooking utensil is appropriate to the type and size of the stove.

- Concentrate the heat under the pot with a windscreen. Be sure there is proper ventilation for the flame and the fuel tank.

- Insulate the stove from the cold ground. (You can obtain closed cell foam insulation, for this purpose, from a camping supply store.)

Types of Outdoor Cooking

The following types of cooking can be done outdoors.

Toasting is browning over a bed of coals.

Broiling is cooking over coals. Turn the food and let it cook slowly. Food can be broiled on a stick, on a wire rack, or in a pan. To pan broil, heat the frying pan first; turn the meat often, pouring off the fat so the meat does not fry.

Stewing or Boiling is cooking in water or liquid. To stew, brown the meat first, then cook slowly in water until the meat is tender; cover the pot and keep the fire going for several hours.

Frying is cooking food by browning or searing in a pan with a little cooking oil or fat. You will need a bed of hot coals for this kind of cooking.

Steaming is cooking by steam with little or no moisture added to the food.

The following types of cooking will require a wood or charcoal fire.

Baking is done over coals in a Dutch oven, in a cardboard box oven, in a foil packet, in a reflector oven, or on the end of a green stick, that is, a stick that does not snap when bent.

Planking is done by fastening fish or meat to a board and cooking the meat by reflected heat.

Barbecuing is roasting meat over coals (sometimes while basting with a sauce).

Bean holes provide continuous heat over a long time without keeping the fire going. To make a bean hole, dig a hole 30 centimeters (12 inches) deeper and wider than your covered pot. (Check the hole for roots. A root fire can go undetected for days.) Line the sides and bottom of the hole with hard, dense rocks that have no holes or cracks. Then build a fire in the hole and keep it going until a deep bed of coals is formed. Put the tightly covered pot in the hole and pack the coals around and over it. Cover the hole with a layer of dirt so the steam and heat cannot escape. It usually takes four to six hours to cook food in a bean hole.

Exploring the Out-of-Doors

Once you and the girls have settled into the campsite and have sampled some great outdoor cooking, you're ready to explore the environment. *Exploring Wildlife Communities with Children*, a GSUSA publication, is an excellent resource for leaders. It introduces readers to ecological concepts and provides ways for adults and children to discover, share, understand, and appreciate the environment.

Trail Signs

The troop may be interested in learning about and using trail signs while exploring the out-of-doors. Trail signs are used to mark paths for others to follow. While on a hike, the girls may want to leave a message so another group can find them. Sticks, stones, twigs, or anything handy may be used. In an emergency, you might even use cloth strips. If a trail is not to be used again, remove any signs the group has created.

Some useful trail signs are:

Keep Going

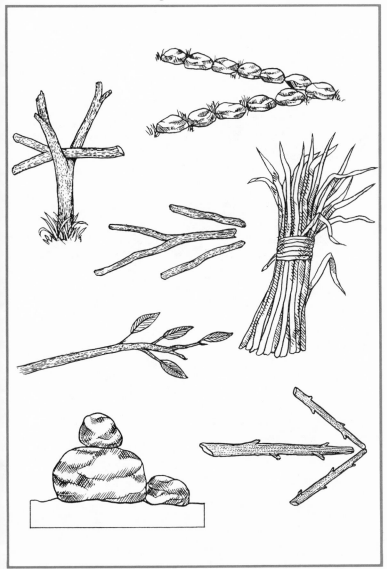

Turn Right

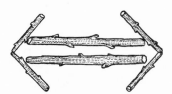

Split Your Group

Turn Around and Go Back

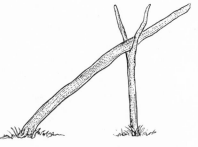

Long Distance This Way

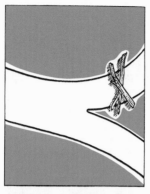

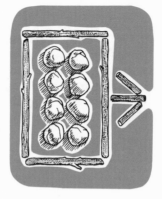

Go Eight Steps This Way

Camp Is This Way

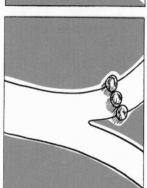

Stop. Go the Other Way

Danger

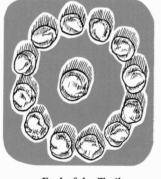

End of the Trail

Wait Here for Next Directions

Girls can make up and agree upon their own trail sign language and lay trails for each other to follow.

Exploration Tools

As the girls' skills develop, the environment can be explored using the compass, maps, the sun, or the stars as exploration tools.

To begin, find out which way is North. If you know which direction is North, you can find the other directions easily. When you're facing North, East is to your right, West is to your left, and South is behind you.

The sun can indicate general directions. In the morning, the sun rises in the East. To locate approximate North, turn your right shoulder toward the early morning sun and you will be facing North.

EAST

NORTH

In the late afternoon, the sun is in the West. To locate approximate North, turn your left shoulder toward the sun and you will be facing North.

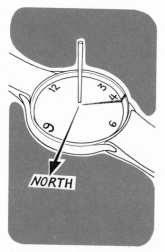

On a sunny day, a wristwatch can be used to find North. Hold the watch level in the sun. Hold a tiny stick vertically over the center point of the watch so a shadow falls on the watch face. Rotate the watch until the shadow lies over the hour hand. North is the point halfway between the hour hand and the number 12 going the shortest way around the face of the watch.

On a clear night, the North Star will show you where North is. Since the North Star is not a particularly bright star, use the two "pointer stars" of the Big Dipper to help locate the North Star. (See The World of Today and Tomorrow in the Outdoor Education Activities section of this book for more details on finding the North Star.) By facing the North Star, you will be looking North. Once the North Star has been located, other directions can be found.

The Compass

A compass determines direction with a steel needle attracted by the magnetism of the Earth. When at rest, the needle points to the north end of this giant magnet. (Note that the magnetic North Pole of the Earth is considered true-North and is different from the geographic North indicated on most maps.) Be careful not to hold the compass close to anything that might have magnetic properties or the needle will point toward the object and not toward North.

The letters on a compass are N for North, E for East, S for South, and W for West. To orient a compass to North, hold it level in front of you and turn the compass housing until the N on the compass lines up with the tip of the compass needle.

When North is located, East, West, South, and all the points in between can then be located. The points between N and E are NNE, NE, and ENE. Learn all the points on the compass, starting at N and going all the way around the N again. This is called boxing the compass.

The numbers on a compass are called degrees or bearings. A compass has 360 degrees, indicated by the symbol °. 90° is the same as East. What direction would 315° be?

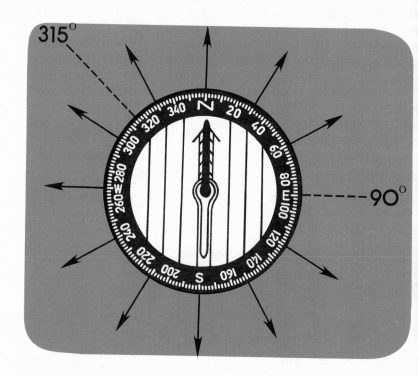

The following terms may be useful when working with a compass.

Direction-of-travel arrow—points in the direction to go after the compass is set.

Cardinal points—North, South, East, West.

Magnetized needle—moves inside the compass housing and always points North when at rest.

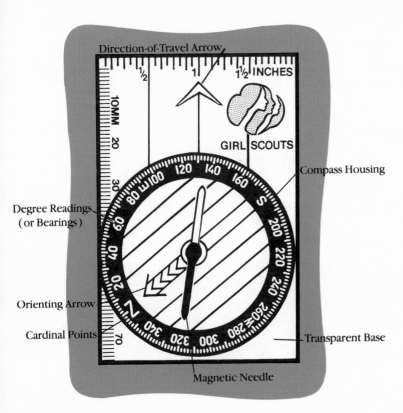

Direction-of-Travel Arrow

½ 1 1½ INCHES

10MM 20

GIRL SCOUTS

120 140 160

80 W 100

S

Compass Housing

60

Degree Readings
(or Bearings)

40

200
220
240

20

260 E 280

N

Orienting Arrow

Cardinal Points 70

300 320 340

Transparent Base

Magnetic Needle

Degree readings—360 directions you can travel from any point.

Ordinal or intercardinal points—Northeast, Northwest, Southwest, Southeast.

Transparent base—shows direction-of-travel arrow and a scale of millimeters and inches for computing distance on a map.

Compass housing—"houses" the needle.

Orienting arrow—stationary arrow inside the housing.

USING THE COMPASS TO FOLLOW DIRECTION

To travel 270° or head West: Turn the compass housing until 270° is in line with the direction-of-travel arrow. Hold the compass level in your hand with the direction-of-travel arrow pointing straight ahead of you.

Orient the compass by turning your body until the orienting arrow is right underneath the magnetic needle and pointing in the same direction. The direction you are now facing is 270°W. Site a landmark in the distance in line with the direction of the travel arrow. You will be walking West as you walk toward that landmark.

FINDING DIRECTION USING THE COMPASS

To check the degree reading for a landmark, hold the compass level with the direction-of-travel arrow pointing toward the landmark. Turn the compass housing until the orienting arrow is directly under the magnetic needle and points in the same direction. The degree reading for the landmark is lined up with the direction-of-travel arrow.

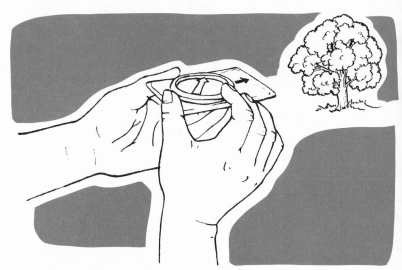

Maps

Familiarize yourself with maps before camping by studying a local road or city street map. Locate familiar landmarks and determine where you are on the map.

Topographical maps provide additional information about the contours and surface features of an area. Obtain a topographical map of the outdoor area your troop will be visiting. Study the details of terrain. Note that the closer together the contour lines, the steeper the terrain. Colors symbolize particular features, such as blue for water, green for trees, and brown for land features.

Orient the map by turning it until the map's North points in the same direction as the compass's magnetic needle. If you traveled due South from your location, what would you see? Explore the map, sighting landmarks with your compass along the way. If you traveled East 120°, what would you see? Practice map reading by making up questions that can be answered by using the map.

Village		Telephone	– – – – – –
School		Power Line	•–––•–––•–––•
Church		Open Pit or Quarry	
Railroad		Lake (Blue)	
Hard-Surfaced Road		Sand	
Improved Road		Marsh	
Unimproved Road	= = = = = = =	Woods	
Trail		River (Blue)	
Bridges		Hill Contours	

Using a Map and a Compass

Orient the map to North by turning the map (with the compass on it) around slowly until the magnetic needle rests over the orienting arrow, pointing to N.

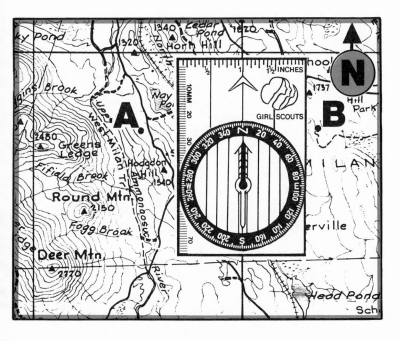

Suppose you wish to go from point A to point B. Place the edge of the plastic base of the compass along the line of travel from A to B, with the direction-of-travel arrow pointing toward B.

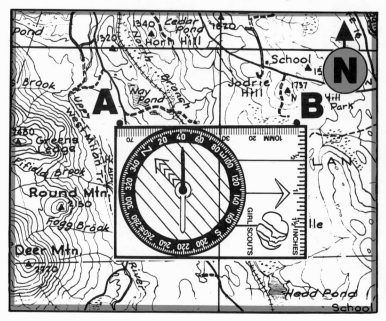

Turn the compass housing until the orienting arrow points North, parallel with the meridian (vertical) lines on the map. (Disregard the magnetic needle during this operation.)

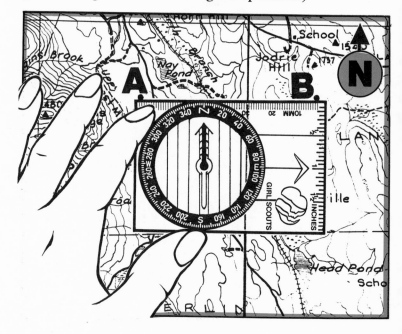

The degree reading for point B lies along the direction-of-travel arrow.

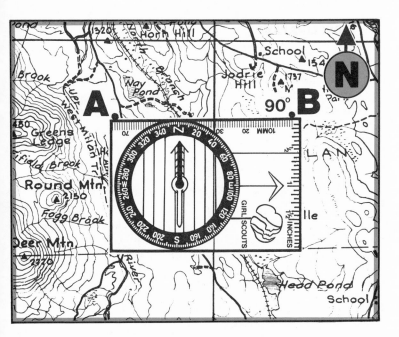

To calculate distance, first measure the distance between point A to point B with the millimeter (inch) rule on the plastic base of the compass.

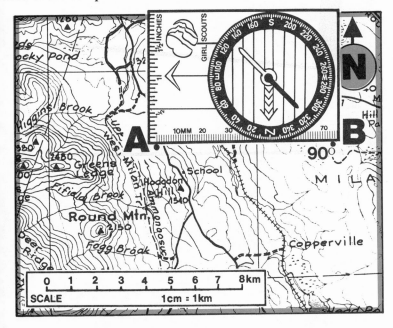

Then check the map scale in the margin to convert map measurement to meters (feet) or kilometers (miles) for the distance between point A and point B.

DECLINATION

Declination is the angle between the direction the compass needle points (magnetic-North) and the geographic or true-North Pole of the Earth. Geographic or true-North and magnetic-North are not the same place; geographic or true-North indicated on most maps is the point on the Earth's surface below the North Star. The compass needle does not point to this geographic North.

It is important to ascertain the local declination because your intended course will not be correct if you depend on a compass direction taken from a map without considering the declination. The declination can be found on the margin of a map or from city engineers.

Let's say the degree of declination where you live is 5° W and the compass reading for your destination is 282°. Add 5 to 282 and get 287°. Reset the direction-of-travel arrow at 287° (by turning the compass housing) and you are ready to proceed.

If your declination is East, subtract the degree of declination from the compass reading for your destination. For example, if the degree of declination where you live is 10° E and the compass reading for where you're going is 144°, you will need to reset the compass to 134° (10° subtracted from 144°).

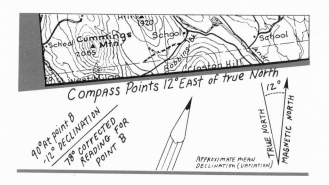

An easy way to remember this information is to memorize this rhyme:

Declination West—Compass Best
Declination East—Compass Least

Something that's been added to is best. Subtraction makes things less by reducing to the least amount.

When hiking with a map and a compass:

1. Establish the direction of your destination, for example, 95°.

2. Set your compass and remember to correct for declination.

3. Face the direction of travel. Look for (sight) a landmark in the distance (tree, large rock, etc.) in the direction of point B.

Point B

4. Walk to the landmark.

5. When you reach this first landmark, sight along the direction-of-travel arrow on the compass to find another landmark along the route to your destination. Continue in this way.

6. To go around obstacles (with no landmarks ahead):

a. Turn at a right angle to your intended course and count your paces. (A pace is the distance covered in two steps.)

b. Walk a parallel course to your intended route.

c. Turn at a right angle again and return to your course with the same number of paces counted.

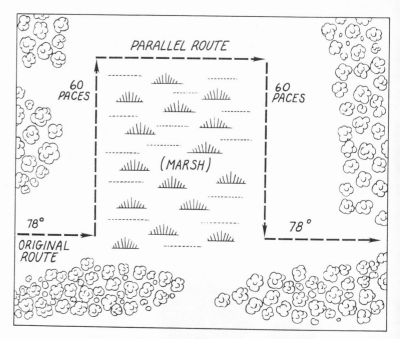

Backsighting: To determine that you are on the right course, "backsight" the last landmark. With the direction-of-travel arrow still set for your intended course, turn your body around until the south end of the magnetic needle settles over the north end of the orienting arrow. If the direction-of-travel arrow now points toward your last landmark, you are on course.

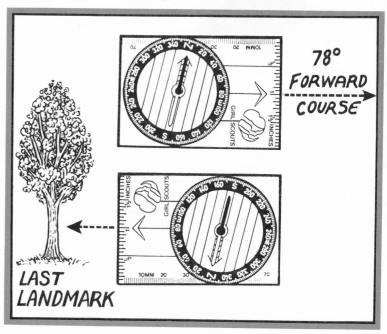

Sketch Maps

A sketch map is a simple handdrawn map that can be used to help you remember your route or to direct someone to a certain spot. If making a map of a place in a town, for example, show the streets to cross and easily recognized landmarks such as a grocery store, a vacant lot, or a stoplight. Add walking time if known.

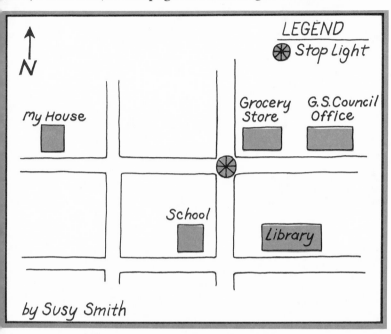

When there is not enough room on the map to include all the information needed, use symbols to represent features such as a hiking trail, stream, or building. The symbols should be explained in the legend, which can be placed in a corner of the map.

DETERMINING DISTANCE

One of the first steps in mapmaking is to learn to estimate the distance traveled. This is done by determining the length of your steps and counting the steps taken. The easiest way to do this is to determine the length of your pace (the distance you cover in two steps). Here's how to determine the length of your pace:

1. Mark off a pace course by driving a stake into the ground at each end of the measured distance (30 meters [100 feet], for example).

2. Walk from one end of the course to the other in your normal stride. Count the number of paces taken. (Count each time you put down your right foot or left, whichever is preferred.)

3. Repeat two more times.

4. Add together the number of paces taken each time and divide by three to get the average number of paces taken in the measured distance.

For example:

Metric	U. S. Equivalent
On a 30-meter pace course	On a 100-foot pace course
20 paces	21 paces
22 paces	19 paces
+ 18 paces	+ 20 paces
60 paces	60 paces
60 ÷ 3 paces = 20 paces (average number)	60 ÷ 3 paces = 20 paces (average number)

5. To find the length of the average pace, divide the distance by the average number of paces.

$$\frac{\text{Distance}}{\text{Average number of paces}} = \text{Length of average pace}$$

For example:

Metric	U. S. Equivalent
$\frac{30 \text{ meters}}{20 \text{ paces}} = 1.5$ meters per pace	$\frac{100 \text{ feet}}{20 \text{ paces}} = 5$ feet per pace

It is important to remember the length of your pace. Now you can estimate distance whenever you wish. Simply count the number of paces it takes to cover an unknown distance and multiply this by the length of your pace.

For example:

Metric	U. S. Equivalent
93 paces x 1.5 meters per pace = 139.5 meters traveled	75 paces x 5 feet per pace = 375 feet traveled

To make a sketch map, follow these steps:

1. Select an area for mapping. Establish a starting point at or near a clearly recognizable feature.

2. Take field notes describing the direction, distance, and features for each leg of your path. Note the degree reading on the compass for each direction of travel. Count the number of paces between landmarks. Document this information in an orderly way.

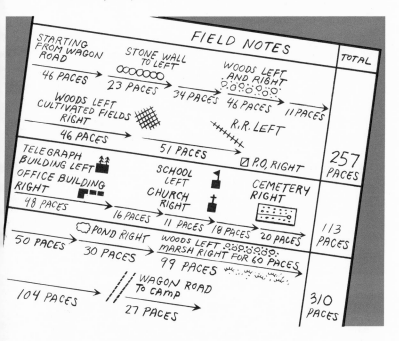

3. Before drawing the map:

a. Transcribe the field notes.

b. Change paces into distance traveled (multiply the number of paces counted by the length of your pace).

c. Select a map scale so land distances will fit into the size paper being used.

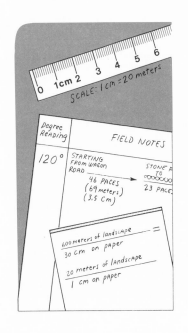

Metric	U. S. Equivalent
If 600 meters of landscape are to be represented on a piece of paper 30 centimeters wide, each centimeter on the map could represent 20 meters of distance traveled.	If 100 feet of landscape must fit on a 12-inch piece of paper, one inch on the map could represent ten feet of the distance traveled.
Scale: 1 centimeter = 20 meters	*Scale:* 1 inch = 10 feet

d. Change the distance traveled to map measurement.

4. Draw the map.

a. On a large sheet of paper, label the top edge NORTH and draw a North directional arrow in the corner. Draw vertical guidelines to represent N-S lines. Turn the paper around slowly, with the compass on it, until the magnetic needle points to North. Do not move your paper from this position during the following steps. (You may want to tape down the corners.)

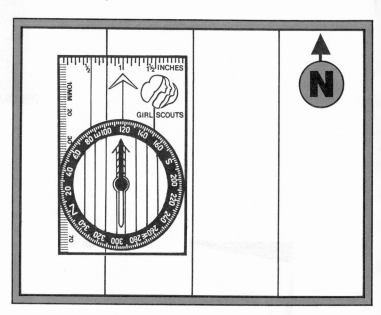

b. Turn the compass housing to line up the direction-of-travel arrow with the first degree reading from the field notes.

c. Place the compass on the paper with the orienting arrow parallel to the N-S lines and pointing toward the map's North.

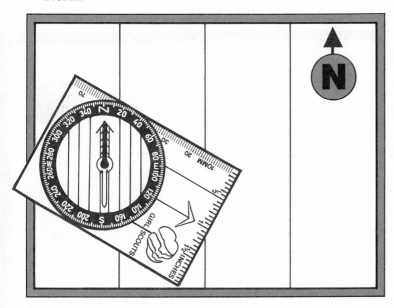

d. Mark an "X" on the paper to indicate the starting point. Draw a line along the long side of the compass base. This line represents the direction you traveled during the first leg of your path.

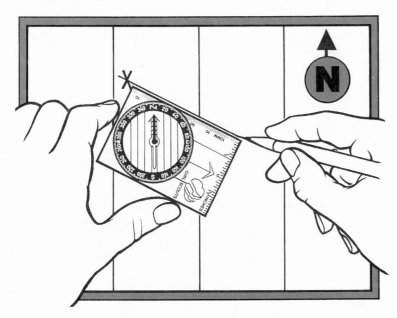

e. Make the line equal in length to the scale distance for the first segment of your path.
f. Add landmarks to the map at the correct places, as noted in your field notes.

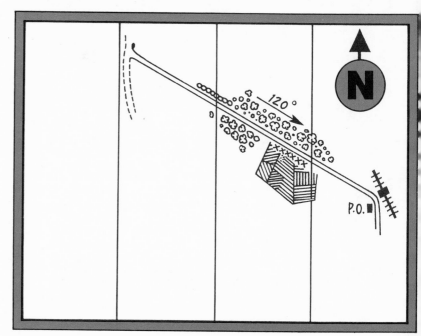

g. Complete the map by joining line segments that represent sections of the path traveled.
h. In the map legend, note the scale used and identify any symbols. Add the name of the mapmakers, the date made, and the location of the map. Names of places can be added where appropriate to help a map user locate the setting and features of the map.

Girl Scout Ceremonies

Ceremonies have always been an integral part of Girl Scouting and are designed to enrich events and special occasions. Investitures, rededications, and Court of Awards are just a few of the many ceremonies that have marked meaningful moments in Girl Scouting.

This section discusses Girl Scout ceremonies in the out-of-doors. Using the concept of progression in outdoor ceremonies, leaders can help girls learn to plan and conduct outdoor ceremonies, flag ceremonies, and a Girl Scouts' Own in a natural setting.

Outdoor Ceremonies

Picture a northern autumnal setting, with leaves gold and red, as the site for a meaningful investiture ceremony for Brownie or Junior Girl Scouts. Or imagine the backdrop of a western mountain range for a Court of Awards where Cadette Girl Scouts receive the recognitions for which they have worked so hard. The out-of-doors can provide the perfect setting for all Girl Scout ceremonies. Indeed, it can add the magic spark of which memories are made.

As with all activities in Girl Scouting, progression plays a key role in helping girls develop to their full potential. Start with small, simple ceremonies and as confidence and skill develop, girls will be able to plan larger, more complex ceremonies.

Progression provides an opportunity to strengthen the girl/adult partnership so that communication continues as the girls take on increased responsibility for planning and carrying out events.

Simple Troop Ceremonies

Performing the troop's opening or closing ceremony in the out-of-doors is an excellent way to link the out-of-doors to Girl Scout ceremonies. An easily accessible area near where the troop meets or a local park or beach are ideal places to begin simple troop ceremonies. Flag ceremonies, investitures, Court of Awards ceremonies, Thinking Day celebrations, and other Girl Scout ceremonies also can be enhanced by the beauty of a natural setting.

Neighborhood or Intertroop Ceremonies

Plan a neighborhood event such as a program event involving several troops, a fly-up or bridging ceremony, or a year-end Court of Awards ceremony as the next step in the progression. Singing and poetry can be added elements that make the event special.

Ceremonies at Camp

The camp setting is a natural place for a meaningful ceremony in the out-of-doors. The ceremony could be a Girl Scouts' Own, a welcoming ceremony, a final night ceremony, an expanded flag ceremony, or a ceremony around a campfire. Girls and adults working in partnership on the plans will ensure that the ceremony has meaning for everyone.

A camping experience at day or resident camp expands the opportunities for meaningful and more elaborate outdoor ceremonies. Flag ceremonies can be enriched by adding historical references, state flags, flags of other countries, the World Association of Girl Guides and Girl Scouts flag (along with references to some facts about WAGGGS), and perhaps some quotations from poems or songs.

Girl Scouts' Own ceremonies at camp can be the source of lifelong memories for campers who, as adults, will recall the inspirational phrases, quotes, and poems learned at camp. The girls' wishes can be written on small pieces of paper, read, and then placed in a campfire to become part of the smoke that rises above the group. Small paper boats or boats made of wooden sticks found on the ground and tied together with paper containing the girls' wishes can be placed to float out onto a lake. Each little boat, sometimes holding a lit candle, can represent a girl's wish. With good planning and preparation, these ceremonies can be meaningful and inspirational.

A potlatch, a ceremonial giving of gifts inspired by American Indian tribes of the Northwest Coast, could be held at camp. The custom of potlatch stems from a legend that explains why birds have colorful feathers. As the story goes, two American Indian girls plucked the feathers of a magic bird and distributed his colorful feathers to the colorless birds living in the forest. From that time on, birds have had colored feathers and this gift is remembered at potlatch ceremonies.

In traditional Northwest Coast tribe custom, families were summoned to the potlatch by a messenger carrying a bundle of sticks that represented the number of people to be invited. The ceremony included speeches, songs, dances, and games. Handmade gifts were given to the guests just before they departed.

If you hold a potlatch at camp, girls or troops might exchange small, handmade gifts that mean something special to them. The potlatch also may involve giving a gift of service to the camp in the way of an organized cleanup or flower planting.

Large-Scale Ceremonies

After planning and conducting several small ceremonies, the girls may be ready for a large, well-organized ceremony for a council event or a wider opportunity. The same elements involved in planning neighborhood or intertroop ceremonies go into planning large-scale outdoor events with some additional considerations. A large outdoor ceremony may require, for instance, a sound system or a raised platform.

An important council event should be well planned and well rehearsed. Plans should be realistic in terms of what the girls will be able to do well. In addition, the participants must know their parts. Every detail must be carefully checked to make sure everything goes according to plan.

Basic tips for planning ceremonies are included in the *Junior Girl Scout Handbook,* the *Cadette and Senior Girl Scout Handbook*, and *Ceremonies in Girl Scouting*.

Flag Ceremonies

A flag ceremony is an important part of Girl Scout program. Girls should be familiar with the proper way to conduct a flag ceremony both indoors and out. Additional information about flag ceremonies and descriptions of an indoor ceremony appear in the *Junior Girl Scout Handbook* and *Ceremonies in Girl Scouting*.

Proper Handling of the Flag

The following pointers about handling and displaying the American flag were derived from Public Law 829 passed by Congress in 1942.

- The right side of the flag is considered the side of honor. If you were to hold the flag while facing the audience, your right side would be the flag's own right. And since honor is always afforded the American flag—not the color guard or the audience—it is the flag's own right that must be given prominence.

- While in a procession with other flags, the American flag should be carried at the right or in front of the other flags. The American flag also should be held slightly higher than the other flags. That is why the flag of our country is always raised first and lowered last.

- When flags of two or more nations are displayed together, they must be flown from separate poles of the same height.

- A salute to the American flag is given when the flag is being raised or lowered, when it passes by, and when the Pledge of Allegiance is recited. Each Girl Scout, whether in uniform or not, salutes the flag by placing her right hand over her heart.

- When the national anthem is played or sung and the flag is presented, everyone should stand and face the flag and salute. If the flag is not present, everyone should stand at attention while the anthem is played.

- The flag should be raised after sunrise and lowered before sunset unless there is a spotlight on the flag.

- In bad weather, the flag should not be displayed outdoors.

- The flag should never be used as a cover or draped over anything. Make sure the flag never touches the ground.

- When the flag is hung horizontally or vertically against a wall or window, the blue field should be at the upper corner of the flag's own right.

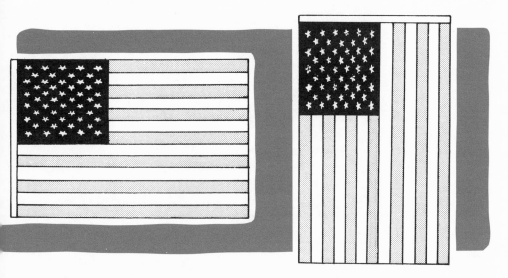

- The flag should be washed or dry-cleaned if it becomes soiled.

- When the flag becomes old and worn it should be destroyed, preferably by burning. Check with the local Girl Scout council or American Legion for the proper procedure for burning the flag.

Conducting Flag Ceremonies in the Out-of-Doors

A flag ceremony in the out-of-doors can add meaning and beauty to any outdoor ceremony. The key to a successful flag ceremony is practice. As long as the girls are familiar with proper handling of the flag and have had adequate time to become comfortable with the raising and lowering of the flag on a large flagpole, they are sure to execute a perfect flag ceremony.

As with all activities in Girl Scouting, a good girl/adult partnership will help the girls plan a ceremony appropriate for the occasion. A short, simple rehearsal with emphasis on speaking clearly, slowly, and loudly will make all the difference in the girls' confidence and consequently in the ceremony.

Formation

Observers should gather around the flagpole in a horseshoe or hollow square formation and stand silently at attention as the color guard advances. The caller, who verbally commands the color guard, should stand at one end of this formation.

The Color Guard

The color guard consists of the color bearer, who holds the flag, and two, four, or more guards, depending on the size of the flag and the number of people needed to handle and fold it. After everyone has assembled, the caller says: "Color guard, advance." The color guard advances until it stands at the foot of the flagpole. The color bearer leads with the triangularly folded flag on her hands and forearms. (The long side of the triangle is toward her body and the broadest point of the triangle leads.) The guards follow in pairs behind her.

The Ceremony

The most important part of the ceremony is the raising and lowering of the flag. Other features of the ceremony such as songs, the Pledge of Allegiance, or poems are recited or sung after the flag has been raised or before it is lowered. The color guard stands at attention during the ceremony. The color guard does not participate in the singing, speaking, or saluting since its part in the ceremony is the handling and guarding of the flag. While the flag is being raised and lowered, all present salute and stand quietly at attention throughout the ceremony. Silence is observed from the time the color guard begins its advance until the color guard returns to its starting point after the ceremony.

Raising the Flag

When the flag is to be raised, the caller says: "Color guard, advance. Post the colors." When the color guard reaches the flagpole, the color bearer passes the flag to the first two color guards to hold while she takes the ropes of the flagpole and fastens the clips to the grommets of the flag. The color bearer should make sure the distance between the clips is the same as between the grommets on the flag. After both grommets have been fastened securely, the bearer quickly hoists the flag up to the top of the flagpole. If the flag does not unfurl by itself, the two front color guards may help unfold it. Then the ropes are secured to the flagpole.

Lowering the Flag

When the flag is to be lowered, the color guard advances as before and stands at attention at the base of the flagpole. The color guard remains at attention until the ceremony is over. The caller announces: "Color guard, retire the colors." The bearer lowers the flag slowly, without stopping, until she can hold the bottom corner of the flag. The color guards step forward to catch the rest of the flag and to prevent it from touching the ground.

The color guards hold the flag while the bearer unhooks the clips. The guards then take the flag from the bearer and fold it into its original triangular shape. The bearer fastens the rope to the flagpole as the guards fold the flag.

Folding the Flag

Open fully, the flag is held by the color guards, with the blue field nearest the flagpole. The flag is folded in half lengthwise (twice, if necessary). The blue field should be on the outside of the fold. The two color guards farthest from the flagpole begin folding the flag into a triangle until the flag is completely folded. The first two color guards then present the folded flag to the bearer.

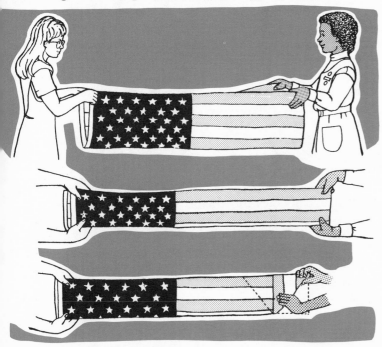

Dismissing the Color Guard

After the girls have lowered and folded the flag, the caller says: "Color guard, dismissed." There is no set way to dismiss the color guard; however, the following are suggestions.

1. The color bearer holds the triangularly folded flag (point forward) and turns right, walking back in the direction the guard advanced. The color guards, in pairs, follow closely behind the color bearer.

2. The color guards, in pairs, line up shoulder to shoulder behind the color bearer. Each guard then turns to face her partner and takes a big step backwards creating an aisle for the color bearer to walk through. The bearer turns about-face, the flag placed correctly in her hands, and walks down the aisle. The color guards fall in behind her in pairs. The caller should say: "Girls, dismissed."

Girl Scouts' Own

Of all the ceremonies that can be held in the out-of-doors, the one most naturally suited to an outdoor environment is a Girl Scouts' Own. A quiet ceremony that revolves around a theme of meaning and inspiration, a Girl Scouts' Own has special significance because girls select a theme that has particular impact on their lives. A Girl Scouts' Own, however, is not a religious ceremony and it should not be used in place of any religious service.

The first step in planning a Girl Scouts' Own is to have girls select an inspirational and meaningful theme by encouraging them to look to the natural world. Sunrises, wildflowers, waterfalls, the seasons, or endangered species are but a few themes from the out-of-doors that could make a meaningful Girl Scouts' Own.

Once the theme has been chosen, girls should search for a symbol that embodies this theme. For example, the flag of our country is a symbol that stands for our government, our people, our way of life. What could be symbolized by a campfire or a lake?

Communicating this theme through songs, poems, pantomime, or prose is the next challenge. Look for books of songs, poetry, prose, etc., that include natural themes.

Once the songs, poems, and stories have been selected, it's time for the girls to plan the actual ceremony. Planning includes deciding the order of the readings and songs and who will read and sing (perhaps everyone); the location of the Girl Scouts' Own; whether or not a campfire will be part of the ceremony; and how the ceremony will end. Allow for rehearsal time to help the Girl Scouts' Own go smoothly.

Steps to a Successful Girl Scouts' Own

1. Choose a theme.
2. Find a symbol to express that theme.
3. Select poems, songs, prose, or dramatics to express the theme.
4. Decide on the order of readings and songs.
5. Decide who will perform each section.
6. Rehearse.
7. Perform the Girl Scouts' Own.

Outdoor Education Activities in the Five Worlds of Interest

This section contains sample activities designed to bring the five Girl Scout worlds of interest into the out-of-doors. While not all of the activities that follow are specifically designed to be performed in the out-of-doors, all are designed to illustrate certain aspects and principles of outdoor education and to reinforce the campcraft skills learned in the first section of this book. Some of the requirements for Girl Scout badges, signs, and interest projects can be fulfilled by these activities. Note that specific activities are set off from the text by boxes.

A good introduction to the basic concepts of outdoor education, these activities can be done at troop meetings, in parks, in school yards, and at camp.

The World of Well-Being

The World of Well-Being focuses on physical, emotional, and social health; nutrition; and exercise. In an outdoor setting, girls can develop strong minds and bodies through mental and physical exercise. Girls can learn to interact with others and their environment.

This chapter will focus on teaching girls how to dress appropriately for various types of weather, prepare nutritious meals, feel safe and secure in the out-of-doors, and become fit for participation in outdoor activities.

Dressing for the Weather

Faced with varying weather conditions in the out-of-doors, girls must be able to dress appropriately, select and care for outdoor clothing, and be prepared for sudden changes in temperature. Dressing appropriately can ensure well-being in cold or hot weather.

It is important that girls be familiar with layering, the basic principle of dressing for the out-of-doors. Layering involves wearing a number of loose-fitting garments rather than one or two heavy garments. Each layer must provide warmth and ventilation without hindering mobility or adding weight. Layering helps the body regulate temperature in warm or cold weather and can help prevent hypothermia (lowered body temperature) or heat exhaustion.

Knowing the characteristics of different types of fabrics such as wool, cotton, nylon, silk, and polyester will make clothing selection easier. For example, wool provides warmth even when wet, while cotton is very good for allowing air circulation (a plus for staying cool).

Light colors are best in the heat because they reflect the sun's rays; select dark colors in the cold because they absorb heat.

To help understand why it is important to wear loose-fitting wool clothing rather than cotton in cold weather, try this experiment:

Put an old cotton sweatshirt sleeve on one arm and a wool sweater sleeve on the other (or a glove or sock may be used). Place both arms into a pail of water so that the lower parts of the sleeves get wet. Remove arms from the water and decide which arm feels warmer.

Cotton soaks up water very quickly and remains wet. Wool helps to retain body warmth even when wet. It dries quickly and sheds water. Therefore, it is more beneficial to wear wool in cold weather.

To demonstrate the importance of warm footwear, obtain several large jars of equal size and shape (e.g., pickle jars) and fill each with very hot tap water. Insert each jar into a different kind of sock (nylon stocking, cotton athletic sock, wool sock, etc.). Set the jars outdoors. Record water temperature in the jars every five minutes. Which jar cools more quickly?

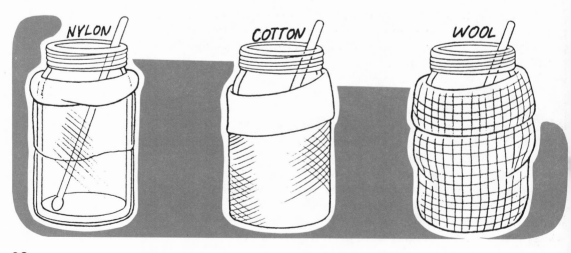

NYLON   COTTON   WOOL

Eating Nutritiously

Most outdoor activities require more energy and burn up more calories than indoor activities. Therefore, plan meals and snacks that provide nourishment and extra energy. Generally, for outdoor use, select foods that can be easily packed or prepared (most can be obtained in the supermarket). Dehydrated or freeze-dried high-energy foods are compatible with hiking or backpacking since these foods are often lightweight and nonperishable. However, the length of a trip should determine the kind and amount of food to be prepared.

It is important to know how to buy, pack, prepare, store, handle, and preserve food for a variety of outdoor activities in different weather conditions. Girls also must be aware of how to protect the food supply from inclement weather, insects, and animals, as well as to make certain that a safe water supply is available. And, of course, girls must know how to maintain a clean and safe cooksite.

Planning Meals

To have a fun and enjoyable cooking experience in the out-of-doors, try the following activities:

> With a group, plan two meals and a snack for a day in the out-of-doors. Choose foods from the four food groups and include only one menu item to be cooked. Plan the menu, shop for the food, and pack. Prepare the food at the outdoor site. Serve and clean up afterwards.

> Plan a complete menu for eight people for a four-day, warm weather outdoor trip. Carefully select meals and snacks that are nutritious, tasty, easy to prepare, easy to pack, and that require no refrigeration. Decide which cooking equipment will be needed such as a stove, cooking pot, water container, spatula, etc. The complete menu is now ready to be enjoyed on a camping trip.

Drying Foods

Drying your own foods can be both economical and fun. Have girls choose, depending on climate, one of the following methods to dry fresh vegetables or fruit. The length of time required for drying food depends on the humidity, the size of each vegetable or fruit, the amount being dried, and the moisture content. Most produce will take four to 10 hours to dry.

Fresh vegetables should be dried at their peak. They should be washed first, then steamed or blanched to preserve their color and quality before drying. Frozen produce (already blanched) does not require further preparation. To rehydrate, cover produce with one centimeter (about one-half inch) boiling water, place in a container with a tight lid, and let stand 10 to 15 minutes.

Fruit can be dried in slices or pureed and dried as a fruit leather. To dry fresh fruit, cut in slices, steam or blanch lightly, and dip in lemon or orange juice to retain the color. Fruit can be eaten dried, or to rehydrate, submerge the fruit slightly in a covered container of boiling water, and let stand 10 to 15 minutes.

Health and Safety

The Girl Scout motto "be prepared" is no place more applicable than in the out-of-doors. Girls must learn to take responsibility for their own safety and well-being and be able to avoid potential hazards by knowing and using precautionary measures. The use of the buddy system and knowledge of first aid, fire safety, accident prevention, search and evacuation procedures, and emergency measures are vital for a positive and rewarding experience in the out-of-doors. (See more on health and safety in the Camping and Campcraft Skills section.)

Using the information provided under Camping and Campcraft Skills, girls should practice in an outdoor setting what to do in the following situations:

- A person is lost.
- A person is caught outdoors in an electrical storm or flood.
- A member of the group has an accident and help must be summoned.
- A member of the group shows symptoms of hypothermia.
- A member of the group shows symptoms of heat exhaustion.

Fitness for the Out-of-Doors

Soccer, field hockey, golf, softball, track and field, skating, skiing, canoeing, swimming, tennis, horseback riding, backpacking, bicycling, and jogging are a sample of the many outdoor sports and games girls participate in. For girls to enjoy these outdoor activities, they must be in good physical condition. Girls cannot be expected to play any sport well if they lack the fitness necessary to perform essential movements. When girls are physically fit, their performance will be improved and their chance of injury reduced.

Physical fitness is influenced by a number of factors including heredity and environment and can be maintained through vigorous exercise. The major components of fitness in girls that the leader should be concerned with are strength, muscular endurance, flexibility, cardiovascular endurance, coordination, stamina, speed, balance, power, and agility.

Warmup Exercises

The following warmup exercises are designed to develop some of the components of fitness, to strengthen and stretch muscles, and to help prevent soreness or injury. The exercises should be done slowly, carefully, and comfortably before participating in an outdoor (or indoor) sport or game. These exercises can be done in most outdoor settings such as a playground, park, backyard, field, camp, trail, or beach.

When performing exercises, do not bounce or jerk—this causes the muscles to contract so that they can't stretch. The number of repetitions for each exercise varies with the physical condition of each girl. Generally, 10 repetitions of most exercises are a good starting point.

CALF STRETCHER (for lower legs)

Face a wall at the distance of one arm's length. Keeping your legs straight and hands flat against the wall, lean forward by bending your arms. Keep your feet on the ground with your toes turned slightly inward. Feel the muscles stretching the back of your legs.

TOE REACH (for back and legs)

Sit on the ground with your legs straight and feet spread about three feet apart. Bend forward, and with both hands, grab one ankle or calf. Pull forward with your arms, trying to touch your head to your leg. Keep your leg straight. Repeat with the other leg.

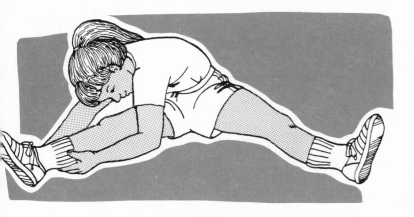

SIDE LEG RAISE (for thigh muscles)

Lie on the ground on your side. Lift your top leg up. Try to keep your leg straight and in a direct line with your body as it is lifted. Repeat several times with each leg.

ARM CIRCLES (for arms and shoulders)

Stand comfortably and hold arms straight out to your sides, palms downward. Rotate your arms in small circles, forward and backward. Now make big circles with your arms, keeping them straight and letting your shoulders do the work.

ONE LEG HUG (for arms and shoulders)

Lie on your back. Lift up one knee and pull it to your chest with both arms. Keep the other leg straight and flat on the ground. Curl your head and shoulders toward your knee. Repeat with the other leg.

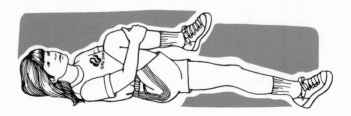

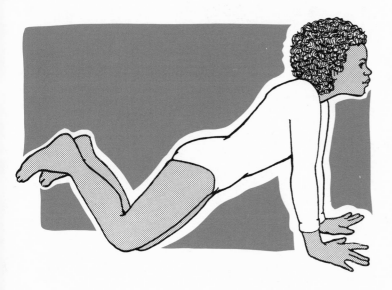

BENT KNEE PUSH-UPS (for arm muscles)

Lie face down on the ground, with your hands on the ground outside your shoulders, fingers pointing forward, knees bent. Lift your body by straightening your arms, keeping your back straight. Return to starting position.

SIDE STRETCH (for shoulders and sides of body)

Stand with feet apart. Lean to the side, reaching down with one hand and over your head with the other. Allow your body weight to stretch the muscles. Repeat to the other side.

TRUNK CURL (for abdominal muscles)

Lie on your back with your knees bent. Roll your head and shoulders as far forward as possible without lifting the lower part of your back off the ground. Return to the starting position. Repeat.

HEEL RAISES (for ankle, calf, and thigh muscles)

Stand erect, your feet 20 to 30 centimeters (8 to 12 inches) apart, and arms at your sides. Rise up on your toes. Return to starting position. Rock back on your heels, raising your toes. Return to starting position.

JOG OR WALK (for heart)

Walk vigorously or jog slowly for two minutes. Allow the heart to prepare for a more vigorous workout.

BALANCE TOUCH (for balance)

Standing with your side to a drawn or painted line on the ground, balance on one foot and reach forward and across with your other foot to touch another line or marker (bean bag, tin can) on the other side of the first line. Maintaining your balance, touch only the object. With each attempt, increase the distance between your foot and the object.

CRANE DIVE (for balance)

With your weight on one foot, your other foot extended in the air to the rear, your arms along your sides and your eyes looking forward, bend forward slowly and maintain for the count of 5. Slowly pick up a small object from the floor in front of you.

Additional Exercises

Girls may wish to jump rope, set up a challenge course of different exercises, exercise to music, or do aerobics as part of their warmup activity. Girls can take turns being the person who selects the exercises and leads the rest of the group.

When working with younger girls, you might have them move like various animals such as a rabbit, bear, crab, or caterpillar as a fun way to stretch their muscles. Encourage girls to play games such as relays, circle games, wide games, or nature games (see *Games for Girl Scouts* for specific games). Encourage older girls to design their own exercises or activities particular to the outdoor sport or game in which they are participating.

Keep in mind that immediately after vigorous exercise, girls should do a cool-down activity. They should continue moving with a slow walk or slow jog. They should not sit, lie down, or stop exercising quickly. As one exercises, the blood supply to the muscles is increased; therefore, the cool-down helps return the body to its normal circulatory pattern. In addition to walking or jogging, girls may do the warmup exercises or design their own slow, stretching exercises as part of the cool-down.

The World of People

The out-of-doors offers a creative forum for exploring the World of People which is concerned with cross-cultural exchange, pluralism, pride of heritage, personal and social relationships, and development of better understanding of self and others. For many cultures, the out-of-doors is an integral part of day-to-day activities as well as a source of inspiration and art. This chapter identifies materials, ideas, and resources to better enhance a cross-cultural perspective.

FOLKTALES AND FOLK MUSIC

Gathering around for an evening of storytelling is one of the most enjoyable experiences in the out-of-doors. Folktales, especially, lend themselves to this setting and provide the added feature of helping girls to better understand the world and its many cultures.

Folktales are special because through them a culture passes on its traditions, values, and codes of behavior to younger generations and newcomers. Sometimes, folktales are written but usually they are told and retold with variations. In addition to their moral purpose, folktales may explain questions of phenomena in nature—how the world was created, why the stars are in the sky, etc. The history and development of this country's cultural heritage are steeped in oral tradition. Folktales about Paul Bunyan, the Mighty Casey, Johnny Appleseed, and John Henry tell the story of the growth of our country.

Check the library for reference materials on folktales, myths, and legends. Films, records, and tapes as well as books may be available. Gear these materials to the ages and level of interest of the girls. Use films in conjunction with a written story to stimulate interest and to help girls learn the tales themselves.

Folktales are universally significant. For instance, in Africa many stories are available about Ananse the spider. In fact, this African folk character is so popular in Ghana that Girl Guides ages 7 to 10 are called Ananse Guides. In Greece, Girl Guides enjoy fables so much that their name for Girl Guides ages 6 to 11 is Poulia—a name from a fable similar to *Aesop's Fables*. Many girls may already be familiar with *Aesop's Fables*. Having girls tell these tales could be an excellent starting point for developing their expertise as storytellers.

As mentioned, every culture attempts to answer questions about the universe, the sun, the sky, the stars, and other natural pheomena. Let the outdoor experience suggest the theme of the stories. What do the girls see in the night sky? Vikings called a star they saw "Lodestar"; Navajo Indians called it "Star that does not move"; the Chinese knew it as the "Great Imperial Ruler of Heaven"; and the Arabs named it "Al Kiblah." Even today in Greece it is known as "Phoenice." Americans call it the North Star. Folktales, legends, and true stories surround this star and can be your guide to fascinating oral history.

Here are some hints to consider when telling a tale:

- Choose a tale you like.
- Be enthusiastic.
- Know the tale well.
- Structure your tale with a beginning, middle, and end.
- Be descriptive.
- Use your body to illustrate the tale (move around, use your hands and legs, use facial expressions, etc.).

There are references to storytellers in every culture. In Germany, the *Minnesingers* were members of the music and poetry guilds. In Ireland, the Ollams were master storytellers. The Incas of Peru had Amauta as oral history specialist. And in Africa, resident and traveling storytellers, known as griots, still practice their art.

The troop's living heritage could be recorded by someone designated troop storyteller. Her job would be to gather, maintain, and pass along, through the oral tradition, information on the troop's outdoor experiences and/or other activities. These stories could then be recorded (taped or written) and shared.

Investigate the history of the community and/or the area selected for an outdoor experience. Try to unearth local folk legends and stories about heroines and heroes to share during the outdoor experience. The local library or historical society can be an excellent resource. Older Girl Scouts, leaders, and family members may be able to help with tales about the campsite, for example.

Music and song provide another means of passing along tradition and culture. Historically, Anglo-Saxon gleemen and, later,

Norman minstrels sang stories. They traveled all over England and Europe learning new tales and passing them along in song, dance, and story. In Africa, music was regarded as a means of communication for it conveyed not only meaning, but ideas, thoughts, hopes, desires, and beliefs.

Traditional rhythms and sounds took root in American folk traditions. English ballads, pioneer work songs, American Indian ritualistic music, and Afro-American spirituals and blues are the backbone of our folk music. Like folktales, these songs are passed along from one generation to another through memory and repetition.

Folk songs include work songs (rhythmic music that helped people work) and lead and follow songs (also known as call and response songs). Typically, these songs dealt with such themes as legendary figures (heroines/heroes, superwomen/men) and tall tales. Folk songs are of interest in the out-of-doors because they bridge the outdoor experience with an activity most are already familiar with—singing and music. And like folktales, folk songs can help girls understand themselves better. Through folk songs, a particular experience, memory, or time can be shared while hiking, walking, working, and relaxing in the out-of-doors. *Sing Together*, a GSUSA publication, contains many contemporary, American, and international folk songs.

> As an activity, a troop can write the lyrics and music to its own folk song to summarize everyone's outdoor experience.

Shelters

As any camper who has had to seek refuge from wind, rain, and cold can testify, choice of shelter is an important consideration in the out-of-doors. In fact, seeking refuge from the elements follows an instinct that dates back to the beginning of human existence. Shelter from the environment is universal.

The climate, resources available, and level of technical know-how are all factors that affect how shelters are built. However, the "people factor" is just as important as other variables. Each of the peoples of the world has a different perspective, not only because of where they live but because of their own cultural style and traditions, which have been the result of time and adaptation. While in the out-of-doors, girls should explore their own feelings and try to recognize others' attitudes toward the environment.

A house or shelter can relate to its physical environment in four different ways. This visual relationship that a building has to its physical surroundings is known as "fitting." Fitting includes:

- *merging*, which describes a relationship in which the shelter blends into the landscape and seems to become part of it.

- *claiming*, which is the opposite of merging and refers to a shelter set in contrast to the land around it.

- *enfronting*, which refers to adapting one face of the shelter to accommodate a particular feature of the physical environment.

- *surrounding*, which refers to a relationship in which elements of the shelter embrace or surround part of the physical environment, such as a walled garden or a courtyard.

Survey the community. Observe and chart the type and style of housing utilized the most and the least. Observe how buildings in your community "fit" into the land. Do they merge? claim? enfront? or surround? Compare a rural and urban design and determine which type of housing is more energy efficient. Investigate how lifestyles affect housing in the community. For example, examine how zoning laws have helped change the face of the city: apartments vs. houses, lofts vs. traditional homes, etc.

Sometimes, need, such as the need for food and safety, is the determining factor in selection of shelter. Some Plains Indian tribes were nomadic people who hunted rather than farmed. Because they moved frequently to follow their food supply, the ideal house for these tribes was a tepee—portable, easy to heat in the winter, cool in the summer, and made from available resources such as leather or birch bark.

Investigate cultures with nomadic people and compare their needs with those of a troop when planning a short-term outdoor experience. Compare and contrast the living experience (housing, transportation, food, clothing, etc.) of several nomadic peoples, for example, African and Asian cultures.

Learn about the cultures that built the following shelters:

Masai huts
Desert tents
Paper houses
Sod houses
Hogans

Another factor that can affect choice of shelter is the length of time to be spent in that shelter. The level of sophistication in design may vary between, for example, shelters used for a one-day stay and those built to last for several months or more.

Have the troop role play a survival situation. First, determine the steps necessary to build shelter in a specific camping area. Then, select materials. Improvised shelters can be made from many things: a few branches, a rain poncho, leaves, or canvas. Finally, build a temporary shelter. (Remember when building a shelter not to damage the environment—for example, avoid chopping a tree.)

Adobe houses, made from sun-dried bricks of clay and straw, are found in Africa, the southwestern United States, and Mexico. Inexpensive to build, adobe houses stay cool in hot climates and are durable enough to last many years.

Recipe for Mud "Adobe" Bricks

Test the soil for the clay content. The best-made bricks will result from a soil of two parts clay to one part sand.

1. To get a good representative soil sample for the test, dig a deep, narrow hole and take a cross-mixture of soil.

2. Fill a container or jar approximately one-third full with sample soil. Add water until the contents of the jar reach the two-thirds mark.

3. Agitate vigorously. Mixture should then be allowed to settle. It should form layers of:

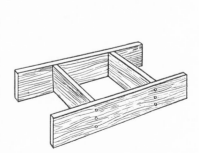

water
clay
sand/silt
stones/sand/other particles

If the test results in all brown mud, this soil won't make adobe bricks. Try testing soil from another area.

Before making bricks, you will need a mold to give bricks a uniform shape. Molds are simple to make. Construct a mold by nailing four pieces of wood together. A mold 25 cm x 20 cm x 12 cm (5 inches x 8 inches x 10 inches) should work well.

To make bricks:

1. Dig a hole deep and roomy enough to stomp around in.

2. Fill the hole with water, mix in the soil originally taken out, and, with a pair of rubber boots on, stomp around in the pit.

3. The consistency of the mud should be pliable but not soupy. Add more dirt or water as needed. Dry grass and/or pine needles added to this mixture will strengthen the bricks and keep them from crumbling.

4. When the mud mixture is ready, wet the mold, then pack it with mud. Make sure it is solidly packed; don't forget to check corners. Level off any excess mud.

5. Lift off the mold. If the brick holds its shape, you're in business; if not, start again.

6. Rinse the mold thoroughly before repeating the process.

The bricks will take a few weeks to dry (in good weather). Turn them every few days to aid the drying process.

Cooking in the Out-of-Doors

In many cultures, cooking outdoors is a part of daily life. If you take the World of People with you in the out-of-doors, meal planning and cooking can offer exciting opportunities for international sharing and understanding.

As you begin your outdoor experience, look cross-culturally at meal and menu planning. Investigate how people from other cultures cook and eat in the out-of-doors. All troop members can share what they know about their own cultural heritage. Interviews with parents, grandparents, relatives, or neighbors can be conducted to find out about cooking outdoors. The stories and ideas should prove interesting. A good cross-section of ethnic outdoor recipes could provide the beginning of a troop cookbook.

> As a troop activity in the out-of-doors, plan an international buffet or meal. Cull recipes from international cookbooks at the local library or have girls contribute ethnic family recipes. It might be helpful, however, to try the recipes before the trip.

In Greece, most cooking is still done over an open charcoal fire; this is also the custom in West Africa. From both of these regions comes a myriad of soup, stew, fish, and spit-roasted cooking recipes that are delicious and simple to make. A Greek meal might consist of soup, bread, and a salad of raw vegetables (greens, cucumbers, peppers, scallions, tomatoes, radishes, and parsley). Try mixing the salad with a dressing of olive oil and lemon juice and then sprinkling feta cheese on top.

In India, food is often cooked over an open fire. Since many Indians do not eat meat, vegetarians and anyone who does not eat meat for religious reasons could consider some Indian recipes and menus. *The Wide World of Girl Guiding and Girl Scouting* includes a wonderful recipe for string bean curry.

When Guías of Peru go camping, they cook over charcoal or in a *pachamanca* (bean hole). A special dish of the Peruvian Guías is *causa*, a mélange of many of their favorite foods—tuna, potatoes, corn, avocados, eggs, and olives. One Guía called *causa* her favorite one-pot meal. The recipe for *causa* can be found in *The Wide World of Girl Guiding and Girl Scouting*. *Causa* can be served as an appetizer or as part of a meal.

Couscous, a light, partially refined wheat grain (semolina), is a Middle Eastern dish and an excellent accompaniment to meat or vegetables cooked outdoors. Couscous takes about three to four minutes to cook and can be found in most supermarkets.

Couscous

250 ml (1 cup) water   250 ml (1 cup) couscous

1. Add couscous to boiling water. Lower heat.
2. Let simmer and stir for 3 to 4 minutes or until the couscous is light and fluffy.

Serves two.

Create your own version of couscous by adding ingredients such as soy sauce, raisins, chopped onions, zucchini, or green pepper. This dish is ideal with fish, lamb shish kebabs, or other barbecued meats.

Shish Kebabs

1 lemon	5 ml (1 teaspoon) oregano
750 g (1 1/2 pounds) of lamb or beef cut into 5 cm (2-inch) cubes	5 ml (1 teaspoon) garlic powder
	salt and pepper
2 large green peppers	5 ml (1 teaspoon) rosemary
3 large tomatoes	6 long skewers
3 small onions	

1. Squeeze lemon juice into a bowl and combine with seasonings. Beat until well-blended.
2. Soak meat in the marinade, turning to coat all sides. Set aside. Let meat marinate at least one hour.
3. Peel onions and cut into quarters.
4. Slice open green peppers and remove seeds. Cut into 2.5 cm (one-inch) pieces.
5. Cut tomatoes into quarters.
6. Alternate cuts of meat, green peppers, tomatoes, and onions on skewers.
7. Grill over hot coals. Turn until all sides are done. Baste with marinade while grilling.

Serve over couscous or rice. Serves 6.

Tabouli salad is another Middle Eastern favorite. Serve tabouli as a salad or with vegetables to make a fine vegetarian main dish.

Tabouli

250 ml (1 cup) fine grain bulgur (cracked wheat)

1 liter (1 quart) water

250 ml (1 cup) chopped scallions or 125 ml (1/2 cup) chopped green onions

250 ml (1 cup) chopped parsley

125 ml (1/2 cup) chopped mint leaves (if not available, substitute more parsley)

250 ml (1 cup) coarsely chopped tomatoes

375 ml (3/4 cup) olive oil

juice of two lemons

salt and pepper to taste

1. Combine bulgur and water in large bowl. Let stand two hours or until light and fluffy. Drain; squeeze out excess water with paper towel.
2. Combine bulgur with rest of ingredients. Season to taste and chill at least one hour.

Serves 8 to 10 on a buffet. To be truly authentic, scoop up the tabouli salad with lettuce leaves instead of with a spoon.

The World of Today and Tomorrow

Activities in the World of Today and Tomorrow encourage girls to observe, classify, think creatively, measure, experiment, and discover. With science and technology taking on a more significant role in the job market and society at large, girls need to develop and be encouraged to pursue scientific interests.

Scientific study began in the out-of-doors. After primitive people mastered methods for providing food, shelter, and clothing, they began to ask questions about the environment and subsequently to search for answers. Thus, the out-of-doors is the perfect setting to explore, discover, and enjoy activities in the World of Today and Tomorrow. The activities that follow demonstrate, on a small scale, major forces at work in the environment. These activities are best done outdoors.

Water

Three-quarters of the surface of the Earth is covered by water. If the Earth's land surfaces were completely leveled, water would cover the Earth everywhere to a depth of over two miles; yet water makes up only one-tenth of one percent of the Earth's mass.

All living things need water to survive. Human beings, along with all other life forms, contain water—in fact, the human body is about 70 percent water. Knowing and understanding this vital resource are essential for knowing and understanding the outdoor world.

The Forms of Water

Water is the only substance on Earth naturally present in three different forms—liquid, solid (ice), and gas (water vapor).

Hunt outdoors for as many examples of water in each of these states—liquid, solid, and gas—as you can find. Some things to consider are clouds, bodies of water, precipitation, glaciers, and living things. Try to find at least 30 examples of water in the environment. Books and magazines can supply additional information.

Energy changes water from one form to another. The addition or removal of heat—one type of energy—is the major factor that changes water from one form to another. Normally, water will freeze (turn into ice) when the temperature is $0°$ C ($32°$ F) and boil (turn into vapor) at $100°$ C ($212°$ F). However, altitude, pressure, or mineral content of the water can alter boiling and freezing points. For instance, salt is one mineral that affects the freezing and boiling temperatures of water.

An easy way to test the effect of mineral content on the temperature of water is to compare the freezing and boiling points of fresh water with those of salt water. Register the temperature with a thermometer designed to measure temperature extremes. Test the freezing and/or boiling points of fresh water first. Then add salt and test again.

You.will find that adding salt to water raises the boiling point; therefore, food cooked in salted water cooks faster. You will also find that salt water has a lower freezing point than fresh water; this explains why a freshwater lake or pond freezes before a nearby body of salt water does.

Differences in Density

Substances found in water can affect the density (weight) of water. For example, salt water is denser and therefore heavier than an equal amount of fresh water. Differences in density of water can be observed in this simple demonstration.

Fill a tall, clear glass halfway with fresh water. Gradually add salt to the water and stir until no more will dissolve. Take approximately the same amount of fresh water and carefully pour it into the glass. To avoid too much mixing caused by the force of the poured water, hold a spoon to the inside of the glass and let the stream of water hit the spoon first. To make this "layered water" effect more striking, add a few drops of food coloring to the salted water before you add the fresh water. The difference in density will be visible. The fresh water will "float" as a distinct layer on top of the colored salt water.

Water also has different densities at different temperatures. Hot water is lighter than an equal volume of cold water. To demonstrate how water density changes at different temperatures, try this activity.

For this activity you will need two identical liter bottles with openings at least 5 centimeters (2 inches) in diameter, food coloring, ice-cold tap water, very hot tap water, and a piece of cardboard or firm sheet of plastic.

Fill one bottle with hot water and add enough drops of food coloring to give a strong tint to the water. Fill the second bottle with cold water. Place the cardboard or plastic over the opening of the bottle filled with cold water. Turn this bottle over, holding the cardboard or plastic in place, and set it on top of the bottle filled with hot water. Align the bottle openings and slide the cardboard or plastic from between the bottles. If this is done in an area where spilled water can cause damage, the bottles should be held over a basin.

Since hot water is lighter than an equal volume of cold water, the cold water will sink and the hot water will rise. Try the same activity with cold salt water and hot fresh water to yield even more dramatic results due to even greater differences in density.

Changes in density due to temperature changes and/or degree of mineral content play a major part in the movement of currents within natural bodies of water. Many basic forces work in combination. For example, when ice forms on a body of salt water, the ice does not contain much salt; the salt is left behind in the water underneath.

Heat Absorption and Retention

Water has a great ability to absorb and retain heat. It can draw heat away from some substances and keep them from burning while not exceeding its normal boiling point. Here is an activity that will demonstrate this ability.

Fill an unwaxed paper cup with water and set it over a fire or candle flame. The cup will not burn, even when the water starts to boil. (This is one way to hard-boil eggs if you don't have a pan or pot.) For the paper to burn, it must reach its kindling point and the kindling point for paper is higher than the boiling point of water. The water draws heat away from the paper and prevents the paper from reaching the kindling point. When the water boils away, the cup will burn.

In its natural state, water is slow to cool down and slow to heat up. The ground may start to freeze and the air temperature may register well below freezing, yet a temperature reading of a nearby body of water may be 5° C (10° F) or higher than the ground or air temperature.

For at least one week, take temperature readings of both the air and a nearby body of water in the early morning, at midday, at sunset, and at night. Compare these readings. Running water, such as a stream or river, will show less variation in temperature at different times of the day than still water. If you are not in an area near water, take readings from a large bucket of water.

Because oceans and other large bodies of water absorb and release heat from the sun so much more slowly than land does, they help keep the Earth's climate from getting too hot or too cold. The ability of large bodies of water to absorb and release heat slowly is also the reason why land near large bodies of water is cooler in summer and warmer in winter than inland.

Changes in water temperature, mineral content, density, heat absorption and retention, and other principles are constantly at play and have a great effect on the environment. After observing these principles through experimentation, apply what you've learned to explain:

- water currents that occur when tidal marshes and rivers meet large bodies of salt water.
- when, where, and how ice forms on bodies of water.
- temperature differences at different depths of water.
- temperature changes in currents felt when swimming.
- how well your body or something else will float in different kinds of water.
- the turnover of water in a pond or lake during the spring and fall.
- the difference in air temperature between shoreline and inland areas.

Weather

Weather is the condition of the atmosphere at any given time or place, and includes moisture, air pressure, wind, and temperature. Tracking some of the indicators of weather can be fun and can help develop an understanding of general weather patterns.

Changes in weather are primarily due to movement of air masses with different temperatures and moisture content. The movement of these air masses is caused by many factors: the Earth's rotation, unequal heating of the Earth at the poles and equator, irregular surface features of the Earth, and the fact that warm, moist air is lighter than cool, dry air (which causes air masses to rise and fall).

Simple equipment will be needed to monitor local weather conditions. Most can be made simply and economically. Two outdoor thermometers will be necessary. Use a chart like the one below to record all weather information.

| Observations | Dates | | | |
	Aug. 2	Aug. 3		
Temperature	81°	85°		
Wind direction	SW	S-SW		
Wind speed	10 m.p.h.	15 m.p.h.		
Cloud conditions	cirrus	overcast stratus		
Humidity	64%	89%		
Precipitation	none	intermittent rain		

One further note about charting the weather: An in-depth study of the weather would most certainly benefit from use of a barometer, an instrument that measures air pressure. Changes in air pressure signal changes in the weather, with high pressure generally associated with fair weather and low pressure with storms. The barometer is not an instrument easily made but one that can be purchased. If you add a barometer to your collection of weather instruments, check the instruction manual and/or reference materials to learn how to use the barometer's readings in weather study.

Wind

Wind, movement of air, is caused primarily by the unequal heating of the Earth's surface. (Large masses of air also move because of the rotation of the Earth.) Unequal heating of the Earth can occur over large surfaces of land and water or over localized areas such as mountains, valleys, and lakes. Wind direction and speed are both important to consider when charting weather conditions.

Determine wind speed through use of the Beaufort scale. The Beaufort scale indicates approximate wind speed based on visual clues in the environment and eliminates the need for an anemometer, the instrument used to measure wind speed.

Beaufort Scale of Wind Velocity

Land Indicators	U.S. Weather Bureau Forecast Terms	Approximate Wind Speed (Kilometers Per Hour)	Approximate Wind Speed (Miles Per Hour)
Air is calm; smoke rises vertically	Calm	Less than 1.6	Less than 1
Wind causes smoke to drift, but does not move weather vanes	Light	5	3
Wind is felt on face; leaves rustle; wind moves simple weather vanes	Light	10	6
Leaves and small twigs are in constant motion; wind extends light flag	Gentle	16	10
Wind raises dust and loose paper; small branches move	Moderate	27	17
Small trees with full leaves sway; crested wavelets form on inland waters	Fresh	35	22
Large branches are in motion; using umbrellas causes difficulty	Strong	45	28
Whole trees move; walking against wind causes some difficulty	Gale	56	35
Wind breaks twigs off trees and generally impedes progress when walking		67	42
Wind causes slight structural damage (for instance, chimney pots and slate are removed)		80	50

Land Indicators	U.S. Weather Bureau Forecast Terms	Approximate Wind Speed (Kilometers Per Hour)	Approximate Wind Speed (Miles Per Hour)
Trees are uprooted; considerable structural damage occurs (seldom experienced inland)		94	59
Widespread damage (very rarely experienced)	Whole Gale	112	70
Widespread damage (very rarely experienced)	Hurricane	120 +	75 +

To construct a weather vane: Mount a directional arrow (with the tail of the arrow broader than the head) on top of a stand that will allow the arrow to pivot freely. Determine accurate NSEW directional readings with a compass. Face the direction the wind is coming from, and determine the direction with the compass. Wind direction is always stated in the direction the wind is coming from.

Air Temperature

Air temperatures that occur anywhere on Earth are due primarily to the sun's energy. (Other factors, however, can cause temperatures to fluctuate.) The longer the sun shines and the more direct the angle of the rays, the greater the warming effect.

The effect of the sun's rays in heating the Earth can be seen by filling two trays with soil to a depth of 4 to 6 centimeters (1½ to 2½ inches). Prop one tray so that the angle of the sun's rays strikes the surface at a 90° angle and lay the other tray so that the angle of light is 45° or less. After one-half hour, take the temperature of the soil in both trays and compare.

Changes in temperature are due to changes in the sun's energy heating the Earth. Surface features affect how the air heats.

Take five air temperature readings daily: (1) just before sunrise (usually the coldest), (2) midmorning, (3) mid-afternoon, (4) just after nightfall, (5) before retiring. Use a standard outdoor thermometer purchased in a hardware store.

Precipitation

Precipitation is any moisture that falls from the sky. The temperature in the air and near the ground determine the form of precipitation — for example, rain, snow, sleet, or hail.

To make a gauge to measure rainfall, place a straight-sided glass or cylinder container in an open area to collect rain. Be careful to avoid places where the container may collect runoff from trees, buildings, or tents. Measure rainfall by holding a ruler alongside the column of water.

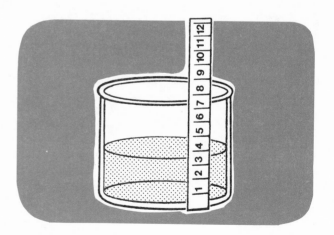

Clouds

Clouds are made of water vapor or ice crystals. The three distinct types of clouds each have a different appearance and are easily recognized — cirrus clouds are high, thin, and wispy; cumulus clouds are billowy and dome-shaped (like mounds of cotton); and stratus clouds are low, flat, and layered. The word "nimbus" combined with one of these terms indicates precipitation.

Watch the cloud patterns over a period of 12 to 24 hours and predict weather using the following chart.

Cloud Name	Appearance	Altitude	Type of Weather
cirrus	thin, wispy, feathery	high	rain may come in a day or two
stratus	thick, uniform, gray	middle-low	cloudy
nimbostratus	heavy, dark gray, flat	low	rain
cumulus	white, fluffy, billowing	midlevel base and rising higher	fair
cumulonimbus	towering, thick, billowing with dark areas — thunderhead	midlevel base and rising higher	thunderstorms with rain or hail
fog	dense water vapor that forms on or near the ground	low	morning fog indicates a clear day

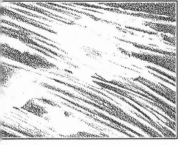

Cirrus

Cumulus

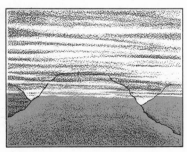

Stratus

Humidity

Humidity, measured by a hygrometer, is the amount of water vapor mixed in the air. The higher the humidity, the more slowly water evaporates; the lower the humidity, the more quickly water evaporates. Evaporation lowers water temperature. One type of hygrometer — a psychrometer — actually measures how rapidly water evaporates by use of two thermometers, one of which has a wet cloth wrapped around the bulb.

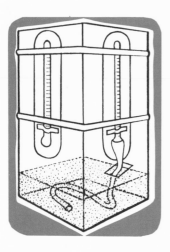

To make your own psychrometer, take two thermometers and slip a piece of white shoelace or cloth over the bulb of one thermometer. Wet the cloth with water. Take air temperature readings with the second thermometer. Take readings from each thermometer and compare the results. Use the chart below to determine humidity. Note also that the homemade psychrometer can be used to take regular daily temperature readings.

Dry-Bulb Temp	Difference Between Dry-Bulb and Wet-Bulb Thermometers															
	1	2	3	4	5	6	7	8	9	10	11	12	13	14	15	16
45	93	86	78	71	64	57	51	33	38	31	25	18	12	6		
46	93	86	79	73	66	58	52	45	39	32	26	20	14	8		
47	93	86	79	72	66	59	52	46	40	34	28	22	16	10	5	
48	93	86	79	73	66	60	54	47	41	35	29	23	18	12	7	1
49	93	86	80	73	67	61	54	48	42	36	31	25	19	14	9	3
50	93	87	80	74	67	61	55	49	43	38	32	27	21	16	10	5
51	94	87	81	75	68	63	56	50	45	39	34	28	23	17	12	7
52	94	87	81	75	69	63	57	51	46	40	35	29	24	19	14	9
53	94	87	81	75	69	63	58	52	47	41	36	31	26	20	16	10
54	94	88	82	76	70	64	59	53	48	42	37	32	27	22	17	12
55	94	88	82	76	70	65	59	54	49	43	39	34	29	24	19	15
56	94	88	82	77	71	65	60	55	50	44	40	35	30	25	21	16
57	94	88	83	77	71	66	61	55	50	45	40	36	32	27	22	18
58	94	89	83	78	72	67	61	56	51	46	42	37	33	28	24	19
59	94	89	83	78	72	67	62	57	52	47	43	38	34	29	25	21
60	94	89	84	78	73	68	63	58	53	48	44	39	34	30	26	22
61	94	89	84	78	73	68	63	58	54	49	44	40	35	32	27	23
62	95	89	84	79	74	69	64	59	54	50	45	41	37	32	28	24
63	95	89	84	79	74	69	64	60	55	51	46	42	38	33	29	26
64	95	90	85	79	74	70	65	60	56	51	47	43	38	34	30	27
65	95	90	85	80	75	70	65	61	56	52	48	44	39	35	31	28

Relative humidity in percent. If difference between dry bulb and wet bulb is zero, humidity is 100%.

General Weather Indicators

- Clouds help hold heat near the Earth, so evenings are generally warmer when it is overcast than when it is clear.
- In most of the United States, an east, southeast, or northeast wind indicates stormy weather and a west or northwest wind fair weather.
- When cumulus clouds become lower, thicker, and darker along with increased winds, a short, heavy rain may follow.
- Cirrus clouds followed by gradually thickening stratus clouds indicate that light, steady rain may follow.

Here are some "folk" predictors that have a scientific explanation and are generally true.

- Red sky at night, sailor's delight. Red sky at morning, sailors take warning.
- Dew in the morning is a sign of a clear day.

Dry-Bulb Temp	Difference Between Dry-Bulb and Wet-Bulb Thermometers															
	1	2	3	4	5	6	7	8	9	10	11	12	13	14	15	16
66	95	90	90	85	75	71	66	61	57	53	49	45	40	36	32	29
67	95	90	85	80	76	71	66	62	58	53	49	45	41	37	33	30
68	95	90	85	81	76	71	67	63	58	54	50	46	42	38	34	31
69	95	90	86	81	76	72	67	63	59	55	51	47	43	39	35	32
70	95	90	86	81	77	72	68	64	60	55	52	48	44	40	36	33
72	95	91	86	82	77	73	69	65	61	57	53	49	45	42	38	35
74	95	91	86	82	78	74	70	66	62	58	54	50	47	43	40	36
76	95	91	87	82	78	74	70	66	63	59	55	52	48	45	41	38
78	96	91	87	83	79	75	71	67	63	60	56	53	49	46	42	39
80	96	91	87	83	79	75	72	68	64	61	57	54	50	47	44	41
82	96	92	87	84	80	76	72	69	65	61	58	55	51	48	45	42
84	96	92	88	84	81	76	73	69	65	62	58	56	52	49	46	43
86	96	92	88	84	81	77	73	70	66	63	59	57	53	50	47	44
88	96	92	88	85	81	77	74	70	67	64	60	57	54	51	48	46
90	96	92	89	85	81	78	74	71	68	65	61	58	55	52	49	47
92	96	92	89	85	81	78	74	72	68	65	62	59	56	53	51	48
94	96	93	89	85	82	79	75	72	69	66	63	60	57	54	52	49
96	96	93	89	86	82	79	76	73	69	66	63	61	58	55	52	50
98	96	93	89	86	83	79	77	73	70	67	64	61	59	55	53	50
100	96	93	89	86	83	80	77	73	70	68	65	62	59	56	54	51

Relative humidity in percent. If difference between dry bulb and wet bulb is zero, humidity is 100%.

- A halo around the moon is a sign of rain.
- Distant lightning with no sound of thunder means a storm is far away.

Astronomy

Worshipped and feared, inspiring awe and scientific debate, the panorama of stars and celestial bodies presents earthbound mortals with the same vistas that ancient peoples gazed upon thousands of years ago.

The camp environment can be the perfect setting for simple astronomical observations. Any large clearing that provides an unobstructed view will suffice. Remember that to conduct effective observations at night, limit the quantity of surface light because light illuminates the night sky and makes all but the brightest objects difficult to detect.

The Daytime Sky

The Earth is constantly surrounded by stars, a fact easily seen on a clear night but certainly not as obvious during the day. During the day, the overwhelming brightness of the star closest the Earth, the sun, illuminates the sky to such a degree that no other stars are bright enough to be seen. However, daytime observations provide valuable information about the sun.

Sunrise, Sunset. The sun does not move through the sky, rising and setting. As the Earth rotates on its axis and spins toward the sun during the night, the sun eventually comes into view. The sun's progress through the day sky is, likewise, not due to the sun's movements but rather to the continued spin of the Earth.

Each day that you are in your outdoor setting, track the pattern of the sun's movements. Note the exact spot on the horizon where the sun is first visible in the morning and where it is finally visible before nightfall. Note the time and take compass readings of the location. Readings taken for at least one week should show changes in the length of day (unless you are situated on the equator). Observing the sun's appearance at different locations on the horizon will give you a sense not only of the Earth's 24-hour spin but also of the Earth's movement in its orbit around the sun.

In summer, in the northern hemisphere, the Earth's axis is tilted toward the sun and in winter away. The change in the Earth's tilt causes differences in the length of day and night. Readings over one month or more will further illustrate this as the sun will be appearing and disappearing at changing points on the horizon.

Indirect Sun Observations

Indirect observation of the sun is very easily accomplished (with homemade materials) and advisable if proper sun filters are not available for direct observation. (The sun sends out many forms of light and radiation that can be extremely harmful to the unprotected eye if viewed directly.)

> Take a sheet of cardboard and a plain sheet of white paper. Poke a large pinhole opening in the cardboard and hold it over the sheet of white paper that has been placed on the ground. Adjust the distance between the cardboard and the paper so that a clearly defined illuminated circle about the size of a quarter is focused on the white paper. This circle is the result of the projection of the sun, not the shape of the hole in the cardboard. Several attempts to obtain proper distance and size of the pinhole may be necessary.

Two interesting solar effects can be seen with the indirect method of observation: sunspots and partial solar eclipses. When sunspots (dark areas on the sun) are present, the projected image also will have these spots. During a partial solar eclipse, a portion of the sun will be in shadow and the projected image may look like a crescent or a circle with a small, semicircular section missing.

The Night Sky

On a clear night far from the sources of surface light, the vista of the heavens can offer an exciting excursion to new discoveries. A better understanding of the night sky can help determine location, establish the time of year, or just provide an exciting introduction to a camp story.

For effective viewing, remember that:

1. ground lighting can greatly interfere with the ability to see. The best viewing takes place on clear, cloudless evenings, as far away as possible from bright, outdoor lights.

2. the best time to study the moon is when the moon is full. However, a new or crescent moon provides the best light for stargazing.

3. star charts and almanacs are simple to obtain and, like road maps for trips to unknown territories, are very helpful for successful exploration. Remember to be patient as well as curious in your exploration.

4. a dim source of light can be used for reading star charts and reference materials in the dark. A small flashlight with a color filter (red is best) will do.

5. binoculars can help you see lunar features. You may even see migrating birds pass in front of the moon.

Stars

Stars are distant suns that produce their own light. Many stars are much like the sun; others are quite different. The twinkling you observe when watching stars is caused by the Earth's dense atmosphere and the long distance the light must travel to reach the Earth.

See how many of the following you can find in your celestial explorations. Some of the stars and constellations listed below may be seen quite easily while others will take experience and patience to spot.

1. *Stars of different brightness* — A star's brightness (magnitude) depends on its size, temperature, and distance from Earth. All the stars in the Big Dipper are very bright.

2. *Stars of different colors* — A star's color depends on its temperature. Blue-white is the hottest followed by, in descending order, white, yellow (like the sun), orange, and red. Don't expect to see strong color differences, but after the eyes adjust to darkness, tints of color can be distinguished. One of the stars in the constellation Orion is a giant red star. And another easily spotted red star is in the constellation Scorpio.

3. *Double stars* — Some stars appear to be very close together, but this is due only to their positions as viewed from Earth. Some stars, however, are actually coupled in space, usually with one star revolving around the other like a planet. The star in the bend of the handle of the Big Dipper is a double star.

4. *The Big Dipper (Ursa Major)* — The Big Dipper is one of the easiest constellations (patterns of stars) to find because all the stars in it are very bright and form a recognizable shape.

5. *The Little Dipper (Ursa Minor)* — Once you've spotted the Big Dipper, use it to find the Little Dipper (see star chart). Its stars are less bright than those of the Big Dipper and it is not as easily discernible.

6. *The North Star (Polaris)* — This star forms the tip of the Little Dipper's handle. The North Star is used for navigation not only because it indicates north, but because, when viewed from the northern hemisphere, it gives the appearance of remaining in a constant place. As the Earth spins, viewers from the northern hemisphere see a change in the position of all the stars in the night sky except the North Star. In fact, a photograph taken with a camera aimed at Polaris with the shutter left open for at least one-half hour will produce a photograph with one central pinpoint of light (Polaris) surrounded by many circular arcs (the apparent motion of other stars).

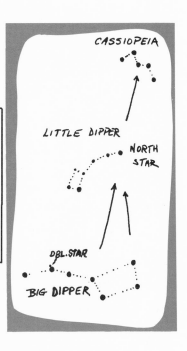

The two stars that form the outside of the Big Dipper bowl can help locate Polaris (the North Star). Polaris is always in the same relative position in the sky when viewed from the northern hemisphere and lies in a direct line from these two stars. Estimate approximately seven times the distance between these two stars to determine the distance from the Big Dipper to Polaris. Find the constellation Cassiopeia by using the Big and Little Dippers as guides.

7. *Constellations* — Use the star chart and charts from other resources to find constellations that can be viewed from your geographic area. Many clusters of stars seen in these constellations are not actually as close to each other as they seem. If you were to look at the night sky from somewhere far beyond the Earth, you would see a different pattern of stars. Many tales and legends are centered around constellations (for example, the zodiac constellations) and hold great significance for many cultures. Use star patterns to identify your own constellations and weave them into new tales for a camp evening.

8. *The Milky Way* — The heavy concentration of stars that form the edge of the Earth's galaxy (billions of stars clustered in space) can be seen on a clear night as a hazy, whitish streak high across the sky.

To find the stars in the chart below, look up at the sky at about 9 P.M. Locate the Big Dipper and the Little Dipper. Turn the chart around, if necessary, so that the positions of the Big Dipper and the Little Dipper in the diagram correspond to their positions in the sky. Match the other constellations.

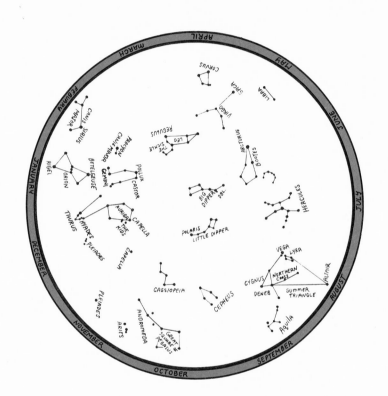

Planets

The word planet is derived from the Greek word for wanderer. Ancient Greeks studied the movement of planets in their early observations of the heavens and noticed that the planets did not move in the same circular pattern as the rest of the stars; hence, the term wanderer. You can track the irregular movement of the planet Venus by noting its position relative to a nearby constellation and recording its movement for at least one week. Venus's position in relation to the other stars will shift, whereas the positions of the stars do not change in relationship to each other. For example, the stars of the Big Dipper always remain in the same positions relative to each other.

Unlike stars, which generate their own light, planets shine because of light reflected from the sun. The three planets listed below often can be distinguished from stars because they have a steady light and do not give the appearance of twinkling, as stars do. This steady shine is because planets are much closer to Earth than any star and are very bright. Planets also move more in relation to the Earth than do the stars. Like the Earth, planets circle in orbits around the sun. Hence, their pattern of movement seen from Earth is different than the movement of stars.

1. *Venus* — The planet next closest to the sun from Earth is shrouded in deep clouds that cause a bright reflection of sunlight. Venus, often called the evening and/or morning star because that is when it is most visible, gleams a silvery color brighter than anything else in the night sky except the moon. The farther north you are, the lower its position will be on the horizon.

2. *Mars* — The planet next farthest from the sun than Earth has a reddish surface that gives a reddish tinge to its nightly glow. A chart of the planets should be consulted since the time of year will affect whether or not Mars can be seen and where it will appear on the horizon.

3. *Jupiter* — The largest planet (nearly 11 times the diameter of Earth) shines a bright white color. Half the time it can be seen in the morning and half in the evening. For about two months, it is difficult to see at all. Consult a chart to help find Jupiter.

Meteors and Meteorites

Meteors and meteorites are commonly called shooting stars, but they are not stars. They are fragments of rock, from various sources in space, which vary in size from small particles, such as sand grains, to large pieces of rock. Upon entering the Earth's atmosphere, meteors and meteorites burn because of the friction produced, and appear as brief streaks of light. Fortunately, most meteors and meteorites burn up completely in the Earth's atmosphere and rarely strike the Earth's surface.

Meteors and meteorites may be seen on any night of the year; generally, if you are alert, you can spot four to eight each hour. An excellent time to view meteorites is during meteorite showers. The chart below includes the names of the showers, the dates they occur, and the rate of occurrence per hour.

Meteorite Showers

Name	Approximate Date	Rate Per Hour
Quadrantids	January 1–7	40
Lyrids	April 8–25	15
Perseids	August 9–16	50
Orionids	October 17–24	25
Taurids	November 1–7	15
Leonids	November 13–30	15
Geminids	December 11–18	50

The Moon

On nights of a full or nearly full (gibbous) moon, look for the valleys, ridges, and mountain ranges that pattern the moon's surface. Craters are dark, circular areas and "seas" are dark, irregular areas that are actually plains, not bodies of water as ancient astronomers thought.

The moon is a solid sphere. What appears to be a changing shape is actually a change in the amount of sunlight reflected from the moon's surface. The diagram shows the position of the moon as it orbits the earth and how we see it from earth. When the moon is between the sun and earth, no sunlight hits the side

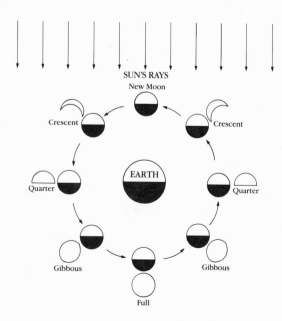

of the moon facing earth; therefore no moon is seen. This is called a new moon. As the moon circles the earth in its 28 day orbit there is a progressive increase in the lighted surface visible on earth. We see this as the moon's phases.

Chart the phases of the moon each night for at least a week. Note how much of the moon is visible and at what point on the horizon the moon first appears.

Special Events

ECLIPSES

An eclipse occurs when one celestial body obscures the light of another. Total solar (sun) eclipses are relatively rare and are only visible from part of the Earth's surface when they do occur. Remember that stars are present in the sky during the day but that sunlight makes the sky too bright to see them. During a total solar eclipse, the sky darkens and stars can be seen during the day.

Planetariums can provide information on solar eclipses visible in a particular area and newspapers will often announce expected eclipses. If you are fortunate enough to view either a total or partial eclipse, remember to protect your eyes by using the indirect projection method when protective filters are not available.

Lunar (moon) eclipses are not as spectacular as solar eclipses, but they occur more frequently. Check an almanac for upcoming lunar eclipses. Since the moonlight does not project harmful radiation, these eclipses can be viewed by looking directly at the moon.

COMETS

These masses of frozen gas and dust develop a glowing tail when they are near the sun. One of the most famous comets is Halley's, which appears every 76 years. During this century, Halley's comet appeared in 1910 and is expected to return in 1986.

NORTHERN LIGHTS (Aurora Borealis)

The northern lights are shimmering colors in the night sky that can be seen from northern latitudes. (In the southern hemisphere, a similar display, southern lights or Aurora Australis, can be seen.) Increased activity on the surface of the sun, such as solar storms and sunspots, creates greater radiation than usual, which can be seen on Earth as glowing lights in the sky. This solar activity affects certain radio transmissions, making communication very difficult.

The World of the Arts

From the stark vistas of the physical environment to the plants and animals that populate the Earth, the out-of-doors has been the subject of countless artistic interpretations. For instance, the French impressionist painters of the late 19th century viewed the landscape, interpreted what they saw, and developed a distinctive style of painting. The theme of the out-of-doors has fused with the energy and creative spirit of composers to produce celebrated operas, symphonies, and songs.

But in addition to providing the subject of artistic media, the out-of-doors has, in many cases, provided the media itself. The first musical instruments were made from natural forms such as reeds, gourds, and hollowed logs. Plant fibers have provided the raw material for canvas or weavings, wood and stone have been transformed into sculptures, plants and minerals have produced pigments, and animal hairs have functioned as paintbrushes.

Artists develop skills to design and create by being sensitive to the environment and to the materials being used. Artists often see things—a particularly interesting pattern or a combination of colors, shapes, and forms—which other people sometimes miss.

This chapter concentrates on development of visual awareness and appreciation of the out-of-doors as it relates to the arts. Interacting visually with your environment does not mean acquiring facts about objects or places, but rather learning to develop a sensitivity to see and enjoy the natural world.

Because certain artistic pursuits such as photography, weaving, or painting involve techniques that can be performed anywhere, the information on the World of the Arts included in each of the Girl Scout handbooks and other Girl Scout resources can be easily applied to the out-of-doors. Check these resources before beginning.

Observing

When different trees are clustered together, they look very similar; but when each tree is viewed singly, the individual shape of each tree can be discerned. Look up into the crowns of trees and observe how different the leaves and branches of each tree are. Another way of identifying different types of trees is to examine their silhouettes.

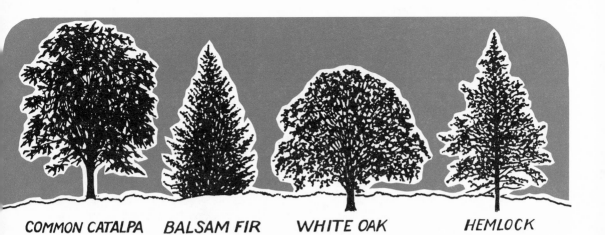

COMMON CATALPA   BALSAM FIR   WHITE OAK   HEMLOCK

A tree can be identified by the shape of its leaf. As you look at the trees, notice that each leaf has a different shape and vein pattern. Drawing the patterns and shapes of some of the leaves can help you distinguish the leaves as well as enhance your sensitivity to shape and design.

Test your observation skills by sketching a favorite plant or flower from memory. Then go outside and take a good look at the plant or flower you sketched in its natural surroundings. Sketch a second drawing while looking at the plant and compare the two sketches.

When leaves fall off the trees in autumn, they cover the ground with a carpet of many colors and patterns. Study the patterns in the swirls of fallen leaves and then look for similar patterns in the world around you.

Create a collage from materials gathered from the out-of-doors. For example, gather leaves, flowers, grass, and twigs. The collage can be a collective project or each girl can create her own. If girls choose to assemble their own collages, design, color, and shape can be as individual as each girl.

Remember, when gathering material for these activities, to encourage girls to appreciate their surroundings and to choose elements slowly:

- Notice the range of colors.
- Observe the different shapes of leaves.
- Sniff the plants and flowers.
- Listen to the sounds the leaves make.
- Notice if plants have fruit, flowers, or buds.
- Look for animals (insects, etc.) or plants (moss) that might live on a larger plant.
- Touch several natural elements (stems of plants, tree bark, blades of grass) and compare the feel.

Also, select living materials carefully. Plants that are uncommon or that reproduce slowly should not be used at all. Check with your state conservation department to find out which plants are protected by law.

Listening

Go outdoors and sit quietly under a tree. Listen to the wind, birds singing or flapping their wings, or leaves rustling. Say, or have one of the girls say to the group: "Close your eyes. Listen to the sounds around you. Listen to the rhythm of the sounds. Make your body move like the sounds. Try moving in rhythm with the sounds. Sing along softly with the sounds you hear."

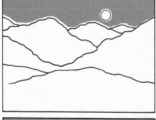

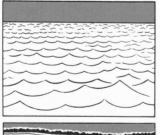

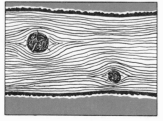

Develop listening power by encouraging girls to pay attention to outdoor sounds. After listening carefully to sounds in the out-of-doors:

- Ask for descriptions of the sounds. If you have a portable tape recorder, record the sounds and later play the tape and try to identify the sounds. Suggest that everyone draw a picture to describe the sounds on the tape.

- Decide which musical instruments produce sounds similar to those found in nature. Find examples of and listen to music meant to evoke feelings of the out-of-doors. Start a collection of songs that have an outdoor theme or focus. Use these songs to enhance activities carried on in the out-of-doors.

Sketching

The visual panorama in the out-of-doors is more than just patterns and shapes. The eye can follow lines of movement in branches of trees, grains of wood, waves or ripples on water, and landscapes.

With a paper and pencil, go outdoors and sketch lines that you observe. When you regroup, have each girl display her sketch to see if others can guess where the lines are from.

Activities for Appreciating Nature in Art

Paintings and Photographs

By looking closely at paintings and photographs of the out-of-doors, you can often sense what the artist may have felt when she or he depicted the scene. The purpose of the following activity is to understand and describe the artist's expression of the out-of-doors through observing and responding to paintings and photographs. Consider conducting this activity in the out-of-doors.

Collect several prints of paintings (or use an art book) and display them to the group. Have each girl study the print or photograph and relate her feelings to the scene depicted. Consider the following questions in a discussion of the painting:

- If you were in the picture, what might you hear? see? smell? feel?
- What kind of place is depicted?
- Which colors do you see? How do they make you feel?
- What could you do if you were there?
- What time of day (or night) do you suppose it is?
- Where do you think this place might be?
- Where is your favorite place in the picture?

Now, go outdoors to a place that inspires you to paint and create your own painting.

Natural Sources for Art Materials

The materials artists use to create are as varied as the art forms themselves. A sculptor, for instance, who carves wood or chisels stone is actually transforming a natural material into art. Art materials themselves often inspire artists, and the activities that follow are included to promote an understanding of the sources of art materials and the inspiration they provide. Before doing the activities, stress the importance of not damaging the environment or destroying living things.

First, make a color wheel of all the colors that might be found in nature. Include shades of brown, gray, and tan. Then, take a short hike to match the colors on the color wheel with the colors you see outdoors. Look for materials that might lend themselves to an artistic project and, without damaging the environment, gather some to arrange in a display (see project suggestions below). Discuss how natural materials might be used in a work of art.

Use natural materials to:

* create a scene, mobile, or sculpture.
* make rubbings. Use textured items such as bark, leaves, seeds, and rocks.
* create imaginary outdoor creatures. Use leaves, seeds, dried ferns, acorns, nuts, or pine cones. Name them and make up a story about them.
* make prints by dipping natural materials in paint and pressing them onto paper.
* create a design on dark paper. Apply glue to the paper and then shake sand, soil, or crushed materials over the glue. Allow the glue to dry thoroughly, then shake off the excess.

When creating an artistic piece, remember to maximize use of the natural material. Try to avoid painting natural objects or changing their natural color.

A good complementary activity would be to study examples of folk art to see how folk artists have used natural materials.

Natural Dyes

Until about 100 years ago, yarns were dyed exclusively with natural materials. As a result, the search for certain colors took on great significance and even changed the course of history. One example is the long search for a purple dye. In the early days of the Roman Empire, the only known source of a deep fast purple (one that does not fade easily) was an elusive mollusk. The mollusk was so hard to find that the garments dyed with its juices became the ultimate status symbol: worn only by royalty, people "born to the purple." By the time the Roman Empire fell, purple cloth was worth its weight in gold, and the mollusk was almost extinct. The desire for this deep, rich color continued. Later, dyers in northern Italy learned how to get a rich purple from a local lichen. That discovery alone was enough to make that region the center of European dyeing for the next few centuries.

By the mid-1800s, chemists had discovered how to make dyes with synthetic materials, and began the industrial manufacture of dyes. Eventually, the process of natural dyeing quietly faded. Even the Navajo and Hopi Indians switched to synthetic dyes. Today, there is a revival of interest in the art of natural dyeing and in the spinning and weaving of natural fibers.

Getting the colors you want when dyeing fabric from natural materials—that is, from mixing and boiling plants, vegetables, or other natural substances with cloth (see following activity)—is a challenge because so many variables affect the resulting color. Thus, possibilities for colors are limitless. Weather, soil, and the season in which the plant was harvested can make a difference in the color produced by a given plant. The minerals in the water and the length of time and amount of heat used in cooking dyes can make a difference, too, as can the pot itself. By varying the use of mordants (substances that make a dye more fade-resistant), you can make many vivid colors from a single plant. For the most part, natural dyeing is a process of experimentation—different attempts will produce different results.

Today, conservation is a concern for dyers. Old recipes included plants that were plentiful at that time, but these same plants are rare in many places now. Dyers should check carefully with conservation agencies to ensure that the plants they intend to gather are not endangered or harmful.

The list below includes common plants and natural materials that can be used for dyeing and the colors they produce. You may wish to create your own combinations.

Plant or Natural Material	Color Produced
onion skins	light brown, yellow, orange
spinach leaves	green
beets	rose
goldenrod flowers	gold
coffee	brown
blackberries	blue
red sumac leaves	black
carrots	yellow
hickory bark	brown
walnut hulls	brown

THE PROCESS OF NATURAL DYEING

Equipment needed:

Enamel pots, rubber gloves, stirring rods (wooden dowels or sticks), paper towels, cheesecloth.

Directions:

Exact proportions are difficult to give because much will depend on the desired shade and the plant material being used. However, the following proportions should give you some idea of amounts. One liter (one quart) of berries, roots, or leaves, 2 liters (two quarts) of water, and 15 grams (one-half ounce) of alum will dye 125 grams (one-quarter pound) of fabric. Prepare fabric to be dyed by washing in soap, rinsing well, and drying before dyeing.

1. Chop leaves, grind roots, or crush berries; measure the amount of dyestuff (materials that make dye).
2. Soak dyestuff overnight in an enamel pot with enough water to cover the materials.
3. Before boiling, add water so there is twice as much water as dyestuff.
4. Boil slowly for at least an hour until color is deeper than desired shade.
5. Strain dye through cheesecloth to remove the plant material.
6. Add 30 grams (one ounce) of alum for each 4 liters (a gallon) of water as mordant.
7. Add yarn or fabric to enamel pot of dye. Be sure the dye completely covers the material.
8. Boil the fabric or yarn in the dye for 30 to 60 minutes.
9. Lift cloth or yarn occasionally with a stick to look at it until you get the color of the dye you want.
10. "Set" the dye so it will not wash out by adding 125 milliliters (one-half cup) of vinegar or 15 grams (one tablespoon) of salt to the liquid in the kettle. Boil for 15 minutes more.
11. Remove the cloth or yarn from the dye. Rinse it in cool water. Hang it in the shade to dry.

The World of the Out-of-Doors

As residents of the Earth, we depend upon our interactions with plants, animals, sun, soil, and water to give us life. Environmental awareness means understanding how all living things interrelate, how to use resources wisely, and how to enjoy natural resources with minimal impact on the land. The manner in which we conduct ourselves in the environment is so important because it affects everyone. Our actions today will be felt by the next generation of Girl Scouts.

The following activities are designed to heighten environmental awareness through simple investigations and games in the World of the Out-of-Doors.

Ingredients for an Ecosystem

An ecosystem reflects a dynamic relationship between living and nonliving components. The survival of plants and animals depends on their interaction with abiotic elements such as soil, wind, sunlight, temperature, moisture, and minerals. An ecosystem may be as large as an ocean or as small as a terrarium.

Ecosystems are complex and each member or component affects another. If a critical link in an ecosystem is destroyed, it may jeopardize the entire ecosystem. For example, a forest fire may kill a large stand of trees. Animals that depend upon the trees for food and shelter will be affected. The soil will no longer receive vital nutrients from leaf decomposition. Plants that require shade will not grow. A new population of plants, birds, mammals, and insects which thrives in an open, well-lighted area will slowly become established. The original forest ecosystem may be altered forever.

Select an ecosystem such as a stream, meadow, desert, or pine grove and investigate all the ingredients. The interaction of living organisms, biotic elements, and abiotic factors is the recipe for the life and survival of an ecosystem.

Journal to Record Elements of the Ecosystem

Date: _____   *Location:* _____

1. *Air temperature at ground level:*

_____   _____   _____

(Use an outdoor Celsius or Fahrenheit thermometer. Take the temperature readings at three different locations such as in the shade, under a rock, or in the direct sunlight.)

2. *Air temperature at chest height:*

——————————— ——————————— ———————————

3. *Wind direction:* ———————————

(Face the wind and, using a compass, determine the direction the wind is coming from.)

4. *Wind speed:* ———————————
(Estimate using the Beaufort scale described in the World of Today and Tomorrow chapter.)

5. *Texture of the soil:* ———————————
(After wetting your fingers, roll the soil between your thumb and forefinger. Sandy soil feels gritty; silty soil feels smooth and slick, like flour; and clay soil feels smooth, plastic, and sticky.)

The texture and structure of soil determine the amount of open spaces or pores in the soil. The amount of open space regulates water percolation (downward movement) through the soil and the length of time water is retained in the soil. Porous, sandy soil allows water to percolate rapidly, out of the reach of plant roots. There is little space between clay soil particles, and therefore the water percolates more slowly.

6. *Color of the soil:* ———————————

7. *Odor of the soil:* ———————————

8. *Altitude — What is the elevation of the site?* ———————————

————————————————————————

9. *Describe the topography or physical features of the site*

(hilly, rocky, flat): ———————————

————————————————————————

10. *List evidence of water or moisture at the site* (lake,

stream, puddles, water droplets on leaves, icicles): ————————

————————————————————————

1. *Number of species of trees, plants, and shrubs on the study site* (identification is not necessary): _____

2. *Why does the variety exist?* _____

_____

3. *How have these trees, plants, and shrubs adapted to this environment for survival?* _____

_____

4. *List evidence of wildlife.* (Look for nests, burrows, scat, tracks, scratchings in soil, feathers, partially eaten food, webs, holes in trees, sounds.)

_____

_____

Evidence of Wildlife

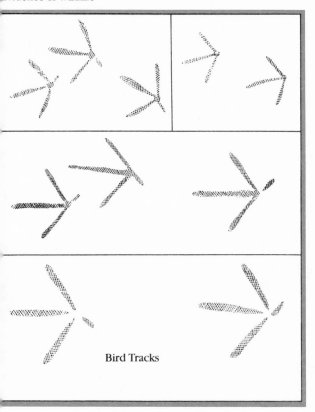

Bird Tracks

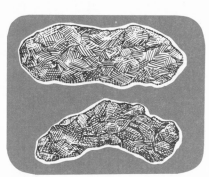

Pellets of Owls
(about two-thirds natural size)

Black Walnuts Opened by Gray Squirrel

15. *How do environmental conditions affect the plants and animals in this community?* _____

_____

_____

16. *Pick three words that best describe this community.* (Think of words that project an image or a feeling for the ecosystem.)

_____   _____   _____

As the troop visits different areas around the council or travels to other parts of the country, the girls can collect a file on various ecosystems. The journal is an interesting and creative way to learn more about the vast number of plants, animals, and nonliving elements that comprise different ecosystems.

In addition to recording findings in the journal, sketch a map of the site to help others visualize your findings. The sketch map can be colorful and creative.

Sample Journal

Date: _____ May 21 _____   *Location:* _____ State Park _____

Forest Ecosystem

1. *Air temperature at ground level:*

    ___13° C (55° F)___   ___14° C (57° F)___   ___11° C (53° F)___
    (Soil warms up more slowly than the air temperature in the spring.)

2. *Air temperature at chest height:*

    ___15° C (59° F)___   ___17° C (62° F)___   ___16° C (61° F)___
    (Organisms can tolerate different ranges of temperatures. The optimum for one organism may not be the optimum for another.)

3. *Wind direction:* _____ NE _____
    (Wind direction indicates coming weather conditions.)

4. *Wind speed:* ___2m/sec. (4 mph)___
    (Wind has positive and negative effects on an ecosystem. Wind can bring moisture to an area or can cause soil erosion.)

FOREST ECOSYSTEM
DATE: MAY 21
LOCATION: STATE PARK
N

13°C (ground level)   15°C (chest Height)
14°C (ground level)
bird nest   wind speed: 4 mph   wind Direction N.E.
12°C (ground level)   soil sample: silty
fox den   16°C (chest Height)
17°C (chest Height)
11m   18m
STATE PARK ROAD

5. *Texture of the soil:* _____ silty _____
   (If the soil feels smooth and slick, it is silty soil.)

6. *Color of the soil:* _____ brown _____
   (The color indicates mineral content, moisture, and organic matter in the soil.)

7. *Odor of the soil:* _____ musty — damp _____
   (Odors in the soil are indicators of moisture and decay.)

8. *Altitude — What is the elevation of the site?*

   _____ 240 meters (about 800 feet) above sea level _____
   (Consult a topographical map to determine the elevation of the site. The growing season is shorter at higher elevations. Wind speed increases at higher altitudes.)

9. *Describe the topography, or physical features of the site:*

   _____ rolling hills, rocky _____
   (Plants and animals living on hillsides are exposed to different conditions than those living on flat land. Surface runoff after rain may wash away seeds and soil on steeper slopes.)

10. *List evidence of water or moisture at the site:*

    _____ soil feels damp, water droplets on leaves and on _____

    _____ spider web. _____
    (No environmental factor is more important to the survival of organisms than water. The distribution of precipitation over the year is critical to wildlife and plants.)

11. *Number of species of trees, plants, and shrubs on the study*

    site: _____ 21 _____

12. *Why does the variety exist?* This site gets good exposure to

    the sun and plenty of moisture.
    (The variety of plant species is an indicator of a healthy ecosystem.)

13. *How have these trees, plants, and shrubs adapted for survival?* _____

_____

(No one really knows the answer. Sue and Juana will check at the library. Nancy will call the naturalist at the nature center.)

14. *List evidence of wildlife:*

bird nest   fox den

woodpecker holes   chewed leaves

animal tracks in the mud

(Since many animals are secretive or move about at night, dawn, or dusk, it is easier to find signs of their presence than to see the animal.)

15. *How do environmental conditions affect the plants and animals in this community?*

There seem to be sufficient sunlight and moisture which

enable the plants and animals to thrive.

(Sun, water, air, and soil are basic to life on Earth.)

16. Pick three words that best describe this community:

    damp   sunny   productive

This activity provides a picture of the factors that influence the plants and animals found at the site. Look at the ingredients of the ecosystem at different times of day or seasons of the year to gain a more complete understanding of the ecosystem. Animal migration, plant growth, insect metamorphosis, rain, or severe cold will all have an impact on the ecosystem and what is observed.

Food Chains/Food Webs

All living organisms depend on the sun for energy. Green plants have the unique ability to make food directly from the sun's energy through a process called photosynthesis. This remarkable capacity makes green plants the food producers of this planet. All living things other than green plants depend either directly or indirectly upon green plants for their food supply. A plant eater such as a cricket shares in the energy of the sun by eating a leaf or nibbling on a blade of grass. A meadowlark may eat the cricket. If the meadowlark eats the cricket, the meadowlark will be consuming food originally created by green plants.

The movement of food from green plants to herbivores (plant-eating animals) to carnivores (meat-eating animals) is known as a food chain. Food chains explain the movement of energy from the sun to green plants to animals. All food chains start with a green plant as the first living organism. When members of a food chain die, their bodies are eaten by scavengers such as vultures or are broken down by bacteria and fungi and recycled into the soil.

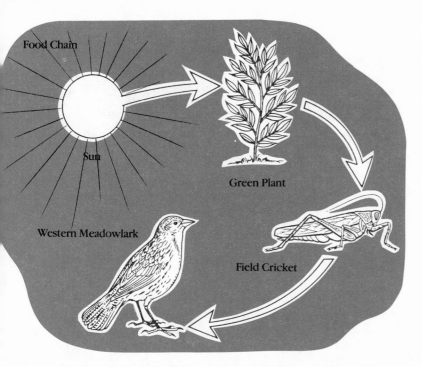

Food Chain

Sun

Green Plant

Western Meadowlark

Field Cricket

A food chain becomes a food web when more than one kind of animal depends on the same plant or animal for food. For example, an acorn may provide food for a squirrel, a bird, a deer, or a mouse. An insect may be eaten by a bird or a skunk. Thus, a food web expresses the variety of consumption patterns in a community. This intertwined, complex pattern of eating and being eaten can produce some very complex food webs.

FOOD WEB GAME

The food web game should be played with at least eight girls sitting in a circle. Each girl holds a piece of paper, 20 cm x 28 cm (8½ inches x 11 inches). One girl has a marking pen. The object of the game is for each girl to "become" a living component of a food web. The outdoor setting should inspire girls to think of different organisms. A marsh, for example, will yield a different food web than a mountain clearing. Each player writes the name of her organism on the paper. (Don't forget green plants.) One of the players holds a ball of string. She holds onto the end of the string and tosses the ball to one of the other members who interacts with her. This continues until a web-like pattern is produced, connecting and interconnecting all of the plants and animals.

When the game reaches the point where a food web is created, ask the following questions: What would happen if a fire raged through this community of plants and animals? a pesticide were sprayed? or a disaster, such as a flood, affected a segment of the food web? Trace the path of the string to find out which community members would be affected.

Increasing Environmental Awareness

Awareness — The Sixth Sense

Can you name the colors of the rainbow in order? What words would you use to describe a milkweed pod or a prickly pear cactus? When was the last time you watched the sun rise? Have you listened to a chorus of spring frogs or the call of an owl at dusk?

We have become accustomed to the fast pace of our mechanized environment. With all the demands on our time, we forget to pause and look at a flower in a field or a bird perched on a branch. Learning to become an outdoor observer means developing a sensitivity to your surroundings and is a skill that requires patience. Development of sensitivity to the out-of-doors is perfected over time. An observer also should be aware of any possible dangers such as poisonous snakes or plants in the area.

All the senses are receptors to the natural world, each absorbing information about the environment. You can learn to fine-tune the senses to appreciate fully the wonders of the natural world. Tax the senses; make them work. Enhance the senses with the following exercises:

- A hand lens magnifies objects and reveals fascinating, minute details that might otherwise go undetected. Using a hand lens, look at familiar features such as the veins of a leaf or an insect clinging to the stem of a plant. Sketch what you see.
- Watch the movement of the clouds as they drift by.
- Smell the variety of scents and aromas in the air.
- Sniff a flower or describe the odor of a trowel full of soil and mud. Have you ever smelled an approaching rainstorm or new odors after a heavy rain?
- Feel the many varied textures in the environment.

- Touch the bark of a tree. Find examples of rough and smooth bark. Look carefully around for other contrasting textures.
- Feel the rhythm and pulse of the land—listen to the buzz of an insect, the wind blowing through a stand of trees, the warning call of a bird. Compare natural sounds to human voices or to machine-made noises.

Perfecting perceptual skills is important to become good outdoor observers. Animals are aware of certain order in their environment; the slightest change brings about suspicion and doubt. These are survival instincts. An animal may take days or weeks to become used to an observation blind or a human camouflaged in its territory.

Kim's Game is a simple activity to practice awareness and concentration and to stretch the memory. Place 15 or 20 natural items on the ground and cover them. The participants are divided into teams. The items are placed in front of each team and are uncovered for one minute. Each team then makes a list of as many items as it can recall and receives one point for each item.

In another exercise, a picture of a natural object is flashed briefly before the group. The group tries to describe the object. The object is flashed a second time so the group can see what it missed. Or, walk through a city park or an urban woodlot and describe what you saw. Walk through a second time and record what you missed.

A Scavenger Hunt—Without Collecting a Thing

In this scavenger hunt, all the chosen objects should be natural. None is actually collected. Awareness and observation skills will be practiced as girls look for and list things they found in the environment. This list should include items that make the scavenger hunt a thought-provoking as well as a fun project. Discourage picking or collecting so as to preserve the natural surroundings of the campsite or park. Hunt for objects on the list below or adapt a list to your area.

Each player has a pencil and a copy of the list of objects to hunt for. The objects listed should be located in the immediate area. Some objects should be easy to find; others should be more challenging.

The players pair off (for safety and to exchange ideas) and should be prepared to return with observations, sketches, and notes about the items on the list. Establish boundaries. The players should not be sent to potentially hazardous places such as cliffs or swampy areas. Set a time limit for the scavenger hunt and call the players back on time.

Now—get ready, get set . . .

1. The softest thing you can find
2. A sun trap
3. The oldest thing you can find
4. Something that lives in water
5. Something yellow
6. Something with six legs
7. A tree shorter than everybody in the group
8. Something a bird would eat
9. A partnership between algae and fungus
10. Evidence of a woodpecker
11. A sign of erosion
12. The smallest thing you can see
13. Something that has an odor
14. An animal home
15. Something natural that serves no purpose in nature
16. Something that always changes
17. Something that chirps
18. An animal track
19. The youngest thing you can find
20. An animal without a backbone

Outdoor Diary

An outdoor diary is a helpful learning tool. Each outdoor adventure can be documented with notes or sketches. Recording events sharpens the senses and develops techniques of observation. Time and patience are important.

Try to allow a few hours during a weekend for outdoor exploration. Start by going outdoors and listening quietly for 20 minutes. Be on the alert for sounds or movements. Be curious—look under logs or rocks, peer into tree stumps.

There are all kinds of opportunities for watching wildlife, in urban areas as well as at campsites. Sit quietly and observe a squirrel gathering food. Set up a bird feeding station. Do some birds eat seeds while others prefer suet? Are some birds more aggressive than others? How many different species of birds visit the feeder? Keep year-round records of the variety of species and number of birds that visit the backyard or window-ledge feeder.

During a camping trip or troop meeting, go for a walk after dark. After 30 to 40 minutes, your eyes will adjust to the darkness. If you use a flashlight, cover the lens with red plastic or cellophane. The red light cannot be perceived by many nocturnal animals.

Keeping field notes in an outdoor diary can be the beginning of a lifetime hobby. Use a pocket-size notebook and a pen or pencil that doesn't smudge to record notes. Use the model outdoor diary below or adapt your own design. An outdoor diary is very personal.

OUTDOOR DIARY

Date: _____   *Time:* _____

Observers: _____

Field conditions:

    Temperature: _____   Wind Direction: _____

    Cloud Cover: _____   Wind Speed: _____

Location: (location on a topographical map or a sketch map— so that you could return to the
    same location or direct another person)

_____

Observations: _____

_____

_____

Sketches:

Conclusions: _____

_____

Wide Games

A wide game involves walking or hiking along a trail that follows a predetermined story or theme. This theme can be based on a folktale, song, poem, comic strip, fairytale, or other idea.

The purpose of a wide game is to learn new skills or to practice existing skills. Activities integrated into the story line of the wide game are done at stations along the trail. The stations are identified by trail markings. (See pages 67-68 of this book and page 116 of the *Junior Girl Scout Handbook*.) Develop activities to be done at each station appropriate to the age level of the troop and the area in which the wide game will be played. Using compass degrees or a code to direct girls from station to station is a good way for girls to increase their competency in compass reading and direction following while having fun.

Suggestions for a Wide Game

Decide which skills or activities will be done at each station depending on the chosen theme of the wide game. The theme of the wide game could be, for example, a story about a troop exploring the out-of-doors, a mysterious hermit who lived in a forest, a group shipwrecked on an island, a research team investigating UFO reports in a mountain region, or any number of other stories the troop creates.

Build your stations around the five worlds of interest. The first station's activities could focus on health and safety skills from the World of Well-Being. The second station could concentrate on storytelling or building shelters from the World of People. Some of the water activities from the World of Today and Tomorrow or exploring skills could be tried in station three. The fourth station could help develop powers of observation and creative skills from the World of the Arts. The fifth station could contain some of the games from the World of the Out-of-Doors. If any materials are needed to carry out the activities, set them up at each station beforehand. Make sure there are enough materials for everyone playing.

Once the story is developed and the trail station activities set up, the wide game outdoors adventure is ready to begin! Participants travel along the trail, stop at each station to do the activities, and then proceed to the next station until they have completed the entire wide game.

Glossary

Glossary

Abiotic: Nonliving components in the environment such as sunlight, soil, wind, temperature, topography, and moisture which affect the growth of living things.

Alum: A mineral salt used to prepare cloth for dyeing.

Anemometer: Instrument for measuring the force or velocity of wind.

Backsighting (backreading): Looking back over the compass toward the point from which you came.

Barometer: Instrument used to predict changes in weather by measuring the weight or pressure of the atmosphere.

Biotic: Living components of an ecosystem.

Day camping: Camping by the day. Girls from different troops sign up as individual campers and are placed in temporary troops (units). The girls and troop leaders plan and carry out activities. Day camping is council sponsored, and the council provides the staff, facilities, and site. The site may be council owned, leased, rented, or borrowed.

Deadfall: Dry wood, found on the ground, that has fallen off a tree.

Declination: The angle between the direction the compass needle points and the true-North line; the difference in degrees between the magnetic-North direction and the true-North direction in any given location.

Duff: Partially decayed organic matter found on the forest floor.

Dyestuff: Material used to make the color in a dye.

Ecosystem: The unit formed by the complex interrelationships among living organisms and nonliving elements in any given area.

First aider: A person who has reached the age of majority in the state where the activity will take place and who has received training in first aid as outlined in the *First Aid Course Criteria*. This may include a physician, registered nurse, physician's assistant, paramedic, or emergency medical technician.

Frostbite: The freezing of body parts as a result of exposure to extremely low temperatures.

Fuel: Anything that supplies energy to a fire such as wood, propane, butane, or charcoal. Specifically in fire building, the term fuel is used to describe large pieces of wood that keep a fire going after it has been started.

Giardia lamblia: An organism found in many natural water sources that can cause intestinal discomfort, diarrhea, loss of appetite, and dehydration if ingested.

Girl Scout camping: An experience that provides a creative, educational opportunity in group living in the out-of-doors. Its purpose is to utilize Girl Scout program, trained leadership, and the resources of natural surroundings to contribute to each camper's mental, physical, social, and spiritual growth.

Heat exhaustion: The body's reaction of dehydration and prolonged exposure to high temperatures. Symptoms include fatigue, weakness, and collapse. Also called heat prostration.

Heatstroke: A life-threatening condition characterized by extremely high body temperature and disturbance of the sweating mechanism.

Hygrometer: An instrument that measures the amount of moisture (humidity) in the air.

Hypothermia: A state of lowered internal body temperature—a life threatening situation.

Imu: A method of cooking food in a hole in the ground.

Itinerary: The planned route to be followed on a journey or trip. (Includes places, dates, and lengths of stay.)

Kindling point: The temperature at which something will start to burn.

Lichen: A combination of an algae and a fungus living together in a mutually dependent relationship. These plants may grow on rocks, trees, soil, overhead wires, etc.

Metamorphosis: The change of body form or structure that occurs in the development of some animals. Insects, for example, may go through three or four stages: from egg, to nymph or larva, to pupa (cocoon), to adult.

Minimal-impact camping (low-impact camping): Camping in which no trace of activities is left. The physical landscape of the campsite is preserved as well as the solitude and spirit of the wilderness.

Mollusks: A group of soft-bodied animals, many of which have shells. Examples include oysters, mussels, clams, snails, and slugs.

Mordant: In natural dyeing, a substance used to prevent colors in the cloth from fading.

Nocturnal animals: Animals active during the night.

Organism: Any living thing, animal, or plant.

Outdoor education: The effective utilization of Girl Scout program in the outdoor setting to enable girls to grow with regard to each of the four Girl Scout program goals. The primary approach should be experiential learning. Through the five Girl Scout worlds of interest, outdoor education enhances understanding and skill development of girls as well as aiding development of outdoor recreation interests. Outdoor education also creates an appreciation of the human relationship with the environment and, while developing skills for creative use of leisure time, teaches the importance of minimal impact to the environment.

Peat soil: Soil containing a high percentage of partially decomposed plants, especially sphagnum moss.

Personal Flotation Device (PFD): A life preserver, buoyant vest, ring buoy, buoyant cushion, or special-purpose water safety buoyant device designed to keep a person afloat in the water.

Photosynthesis: The process by which green plants use the sun's light to make food (simple sugars and carbohydrates) from carbon dioxide and water.

Priming: Making the portable camp stove ready for use. Priming of a portable stove is done according to the manufacturer's instructions.

Psychrometer: A type of hygrometer that measures humidity in the air by registering how rapidly water evaporates.

Resident (established) camping: A camping experience in which the campers live at an established site. Girls from different troops sign up as individual campers and are placed in units (temporary troops). The girls and their counselors or leaders plan activities taking advantage of the opportunities available to them. Resident camping is council sponsored, and the council provides the total staff, facilities, and site. The site may be council owned, leased, rented, or borrowed.

Soil percolation: The movement of water down into and through soil.

Stimulant: Any drug that causes a state of excitation or heightened activity in a person. Caffeine (found in coffee, tea, and cola soft drinks) is one type of stimulant.

Topography: The physical or natural features of the landscape. A topographical map details man-made features, bodies of water, vegetation, and elevation of the landscape.

Travel camping: A camping experience carried out by experienced Girl Scouts and troop leaders wherein motorized transportation is used to move the campers, as a group, from one site to another over a series of days (two or more) for experiences in different environments. Motorized transportation is usually a van, bus, station wagon, or automobile; but it may be an airplane, boat, train, or combination of these.

Trip camping: A camping experience planned and carried out by experienced Girl Scouts and troop/group leaders in which the group camps at different sites for two or more nights and travels from one site to another. The group may travel by bicycle, canoe, horse, sailboat, or other nonmotorized means of transportation.

Troop camping with a core staff (core staff camping): Troop camping using a council-operated site and facilities. Each troop is responsible for its own plans and scheduling, and may or may not take advantage of activities offered by the core staff. The council provides core staff who include a site director and some program specialists.

Troop/group camping: A camping experience of 24 or more consecutive hours, planned and carried out by a troop of Girl Scouts and troop leaders, using sites approved by the council. The site may be non-council owned or council owned, leased, rented, or borrowed.

Bibliography

Bibliography

General

Coutellier, Connie. *Outdoor Book.* Kansas City, Mo.: Camp Fire, Inc., 1980.

Dann, Robert. *The Roadshow Gourmet.* Washington, D.C.: Potomac Appalachian Trial Club, 1989.

Fleming, June. *The Outdoor Idea Book.* Portland, Oreg.: Victoria House, 1978.

Fletcher, Colin. *The Complete Walker III.* New York: Alfred A. Knopf, 1984.

Franz, Carl, and Lorena Havens. *The On and Off the Road Cookbook.* Santa Fe: John Muir Publications, 1982.

Haines, Gail Kay. *Baking in a Box, Cooking in a Can.* New York: William Morrow & Co., 1981.

Hammett, Catherine T. *The Campcraft Book.* Martinsville, Ind.: American Camping Association, 1980.

Hampton, Bruce, and David Cole. *Soft Paths.* Harrisburg, Pa.: Stackpole Books, 1988.

MacManiman, Gen. *Dry It—You'll Like It!* Seattle, Wash.: Evergreen Printing Company, 1973.

Simer, Peter, and John Sullivan. *National Outdoor Leadership School's Official Wilderness Guide.* New York: Simon & Schuster, 1983.

Thomas, Dian. *Backyard Roughing It Easy.* New York: Fawcett Columbine, 1980.

——. *Roughing It Easy II.* New York: Warner Books, Inc., 1977.

——. *Roughing It Easy.* Provo, Utah: Brigham Young University Press, 1974.

Yaffe, Linda Frederick. *High Trail Cookery.* Chicago, Ill.: Chicago Review Press, 1989.

Girl Scout Resources

Girl Scouts of the U.S.A. *Cadette and Senior Girl Scout Handbook.* 1987. Cat. No. 20-791.

——. *Cadette and Senior Girl Scout Interest Projects.* 1987. Cat. No. 20-792.

——. *Ceremonies in Girl Scouting.* 1990. Cat. No. 26-801.

——. *Games for Girl Scouts.* 1990. Cat. No. 20-630.

——. *Junior Girl Scout Handbook.* 1986. Cat. No. 20-785.

——. *Safety-Wise.* 1988. Cat. No. 26-202.

Kennedy, Carolyn L., and Patricia J. Dreier. Contemporary Issues Series, *Earth Matters: A Challenge for Environmental Action.* 1990. Cat. No. 26-827.

Kennedy, Carolyn L. *Exploring Wildlife Communities with Children.* 1981. Cat. No. 19-985.

Health and Safety

American National Red Cross. *Advanced First Aid and Emergency Care.* Garden City, N.Y.: Doubleday & Co., 1980.
———. *American Red Cross Standard First Aid.* Garden City, N.Y.: Doubleday & Co., 1989.
Brown, Terry, and Rob Hunter. *Concise Book of Survival and Rescue.* Agincourt, Canada: Gage Publishing, 1978.
LaChapelle, E. R. *The ABC of Avalanche Safety.* Seattle: The Mountaineers, 1982.
Lathrop, Theodore G., M.D. *Hypothermia: Killer of the Unprepared.* Portland, Oreg.: The Mazamas, 1975.
Mitchell, Dick. *Mountaineering First Aid: A Guide to Accident Response and First Aid Care.* Seattle: The Mountaineers, 1983.
Reifsnyder, William F. *Weathering the Wilderness.* San Francisco: Sierra Club Books, 1980.
Sctnicka, Tim J. *Wilderness Search and Rescue.* Boston: Appalachian Mountain Club, 1980.
Wilkinson, James A., M.D., ed. *Medicine for Mountaineering.* Seattle: The Mountaineers, 1983.

Stoves

"Fire Burn and Cauldron Bubble: Choosing the Right Camp Stove for You." *Bicycling,* September/October 1982.
"Stoves and Lanterns." *Outdoor Life,* June 1980.
"The World's Best Backpacking Stoves." *Backpacker,* June/July 1981.

Knots

Blandford, Percy W. *Knots and Splices.* New York: Perry W. Bell Publishing Co., 1975.
Boy Scouts of America. *Knots and How to Tie Them.* Irving, Tex.: Boy Scouts of America, 1981.
Cassidy, John. *The Klutz Book of Knots.* Palo Alto, Calif.: Klutz Press, 1985.
Hensel, John. *The Book of Ornamental Knots.* New York: Charles Scribner's Sons, 1973.
March, Bill. *Modern Rope Techniques in Mountaineering.* Manchester, N.H.: Ciccrone Press, 1976.

164

Map and Compass

Disley, John. *Your Way with Map and Compass Orienteering.* Willow-dale, Ontario: Canadian Orienteering Service, 1973.

Fleming, June. *Staying Found: The Complete Map and Compass Handbook.* New York: Vintage Books, 1983.

Kals, W.S. *Land Navigation Handbook: The Sierra Club Guide to Map and Compass.* San Francisco: Sierra Club Books, 1983.

Kjellstrom, Bjorn. *Be Expert with Map and Compass.* New York: Charles Scribner's Sons, 1976

Environmental

Cornell, Joseph Bharat. *Sharing Nature with Children.* Nevada City, Calif.: Ananda Publications, 1979.

Cornell, Joseph Bharat. *Sharing the Joy of Nature.* Nevada City, Calif.: Dawn Publications, 1989.

The EarthWorks Group. *50 Simple Things Kids Can Do to Save the Earth.* Kansas City, Mo.: Andrews & McMeel, 1990.

Harris, Mark D. *Embracing the Earth.* Chicago, Ill.: The Noble Press, Inc., 1990.

Index

Index